THE NEW PAGANISM

And Other Sermons

by
William Edward Biederwolf

Minister of Royal Poinciana Chapel
Palm Beach, Florida
and
Director of Winona Lake Bible Conference
Winona Lake, Indiana

SCHMUL PUBLISHING COMPANY
NICHOLASVILLE, KENTUCKY

Published by Schmul Publishing Co.
PO Box 776
Nicholasville, KY USA

Printed in the United States of America

ISBN 10: 0-88019-589-4
ISBN 13: 978-0-88019-589-8

Visit us on the Internet at www.wesleyanbooks.com, or order direct from the publisher by calling 800-772-6657, or by writing to the above address.

Contents

PREFACE

To OBSERVE THAT A PERSON is a "pagan" is not to cast aspersion on their behavior. It is not the same as calling them a "savage." A savage is uncivilized, not subject to the characteristics that are the hallmarks of a modern society, but more in tune with the brutal laws of the jungle. For example, the ancient Romans were highly civilized, with a fine appreciation for the arts, intellectual pursuits, architecture, creative and inventive genius, etc. Nevertheless they worshiped a multitude of gods; they were pagans.

The author of this book took the pulse of America in 1934, and he was deeply disturbed by his own prognosis. At that time, he predicted that if it did not change its ways, the country would become a nation of pagans.

The decade of the 1930s is remembered for many different reasons. Chief among them is the economic stress of the Great Depression. It was also the time of the Public Enemies—Bonnie and Clyde, John Dillinger, Pretty Boy Floyd were on the run, robbing banks and hiding from the "G-men" of the FBI. It has been called the last era of great men's fashion, and aviation buffs call the period the

Golden Age of Flying. Adolf Hitler and the Nazis rose across the seas to cast a dark shadow on American shores. But there were maladies enough inside the borders. The evil seed sown by the Fabian Socialists, Sigmund Freud and the disciples of Charles Darwin sprang up into a bitter harvest. The flappers and dandies of the Roaring Twenties, yearning for the good old days of wild boozy parties and loose morals, blamed the dismal economic conditions on "abuses" perpetrated by Wall Street and the bankers. Trendy intellectuals and academics presented communism and socialism as viable alternatives to capitalism, and Americans desperate for the return of good times began to consider Big Government as the solution to their problems, rather than reliance on God as the great provider, and the historically fiercely-defended virtues of self-reliance.

But after the trauma of World War I and the wild hedonism of the Twenties, many traditional American values were up for scrutiny, and these included the truths of Christianity.

Presbyterian pastor William Biederwolf contemplated the symptoms swirling around him. In this volume he analyzes them and projects ahead into the future from his vantage point in 1934. Chapter 1 is a stunning revelation of his accuracy. A comparison of what he forecasted to our own day in the twenty-first century provides a roadmap of how we arrived at our current state of affairs.

His prescience was uncanny, unnerving and— when applied to the road ahead— horrifying.

The rest of the volume is balanced around the same tone set by the first chapter. Perhaps it can best be described as an analysis of spiritual, civic, social and economic responsibilities of the American Christian, and the consequences incumbent thereon. His Presbyterianism is classic. While not a proponent of Wesleyan holiness, he nevertheless brooks no sin in the life of the Believer, insisting that calling upon the Lord will suppress and overcome all such temptations and tendencies.

It is important to keep in mind the milieu that surrounds the writer. In the depth of the Depression, bankers were often considered the villains, and there was a strong societal urge to seek out a utopian solution to the world's ills. Many Americans found the tenets of communism and socialism appealing, and it was easy for even Christians to decry some of the baser elements of capitalism and free enterprise, such as competition and massive profits. This was especially aggravated during the economic travails of the day when it was perceived such profits were harvested at the expense of the poorer classes of society. With unemployment rates ranging as high as 80% in some portions of the country, there were many Americans who numbered themselves among the poor.

The Founding Fathers of America, while overwhelmingly Christian—regardless of what deconstructionists claim today—recognized that this is still a fallen world with all the attendant troubles introduced by sin. Rather than joust with windmills like Don Quixote, they instituted a system of government and economics that recognizes the state of human nature, and accounts for it in as just and equitable a manner as possible. They balanced the power of self-interest in capitalism with freedom of speech and religion, and an education system that embraced the Christian principle of caring for one's neighbor as oneself. In this way they ensured liberty for Americans free from government interference in matters of conscience, family life, and religious practice. There had been many depressions, recessions and "panics" since the Founders, but the American attitudes of self-reliance, hard work and dependence on God had always carried the nation through.

The decade of the 1930s was different, though. As noted before, Americans toyed with the concepts of socialism as the answer to their ills. This, however, was not the first time in history. Historian Rod Gragg notes in his excellent book, *Forged in Faith*,[1] the earliest colonists had already attempted the social experiment. Independently of each other, both the Jamestown Colony and the Massachusetts Bay Colony of the Puritans had set up what could today be recognized as proto-socialist communities. After only two or three years of starvation and near disaster, the schemes were abandoned in favor of the biblical mandates for individual work and profit, with a heavy emphasis on personal voluntary relief for those who were genuinely in need.

There is a quote widely attributed to Albert Einstein that is germane to this discussion— "Insanity: doing the same thing over and over again and expecting different results."

On the surface, socialism seems rational, well-intentioned, almost Christian in its principles— caring for the downtrodden and those less fortunate, "asking" the rich to "pay their fair share," etc. There are multiple objections advanced against socialism, however. Among these are, first and foremost, 1) it is morally wrong to take the possessions of someone and redistribute it to others, even if it is the state that does the taking; and 2) it has never, ever worked. Socialism has failed every time it has been attempted. Yet, there is a deeper, spiritual objection, as well.

Socialism masquerades as Christianity without Christ.

At its very root, it is succumbing to "the lie" that Paul references in Romans 1:25. He talks about those "who exchanged the truth of God for the lie, and worshiped and served the creature rather than the Creator, who is blessed forever" (NKJV). What is *the* Lie? It is the same falsehood that Satan used to convince Eve in the Garden of Eden. It is the same untruth that he used to seduce a third of the angels into rebellion: "I can be God, too."

---

1. Rod Gragg, *Forged in Faith: How Faith Shaped the Birth of the Nation 1607-1776*, New York: Howard Books, 2010.

Socialism is The Lie put into practice. "We can do this on our own, thank you very much, God."

Of course, the purpose of acting without God is to establish Man as the final authority. Man then decides what is right and wrong. Man decides who will have and have not. Man will decide what is said and is not said. Man will decide what is acceptable and what is forbidden. And Man decides who will and will not be worshiped. (How well did that work for Nazi Germany? The Soviet Union?)

Whether he is irreligious, hedonistic, or a neopagan who practices nature worship, or worships the earth (which is simply the modern interpretation of witchcraft), such a person is a pagan.

When Man insists he will wield such power of decision that elevates him above the lordship of Jesus, then another god has usurped Christ's rightful place. In short, Man becomes a self-worshiping pagan.

I heard one of the preëminent leaders in the Christian school movement make an observation that comes more and more into focus as time passes: "Government never gives anything with one hand but that it takes away a liberty with the other."

At the time of this book's publication, America is entering an election year. Biederwolf speaks to us across more than six decades in the past, and the accuracy of his observations are deeply troubling. Will America continue on the path currently mapped out for it, insisting on Man as the measure of all things? Will it fully turn to the failed tenets of humanistic (not "humanitarian" — there is a significant difference) philosophy, civics, science, religion, economics?

Or will the majority of the American people rise up to say that enough is enough; that the insanity will not be indulged any longer; that we must turn back to the Constitution, accepting the mantle of American Exceptionalism;

re-establishing the shining city on the hill that was seen by the Puritans from the *Mayflower?*

But the issues at hand are not merely about an election; control of congress and state houses; the economy; the military; law enforcement; jobs; equal rights; civil liberties. These are only the benefits and blessings, or curses and problems that are the direct results of our relationship with God.

Such a change of course requires more than civic exercises. It involves changing, not just an administration, a congress, the courts, monetary policies and labor practices, but the hearts and minds of individuals.

It requires prostration of our own will before God himself. The alternative is unthinkable.

Will America, "appealing to the Supreme Judge of the world for the rectitude of our intentions," renew "a firm reliance on the protection of divine Providence," the only true "Author of Liberty"?

—D. Curtis Hale
Publisher, 2016

The relations which exist between man and his Maker, and the duties resulting from those relations, are the most interesting and important to every human being, and the most incumbent on his study and investigation.[1]

—THOMAS JEFFERSON

...Thy love divine hath led us in the past,
In this free land by Thee our lot is cast.
Be Thou our Ruler, Guardian, Guide and Stay,
Thy Word our law, Thy paths our chosen way.

From war's alarms, from deadly pestilence,
Be Thy strong arm our ever sure defense;
Thy true religion in our hearts increase,
Thy bounteous goodness nourish us in peace...[2]

1. Quoted in David Barton, *The Jefferson Lies: Exposing the Myths You've Always Believed About Thomas Jefferson* (Nashville: Thomas Nelson, 2012) pg. 49.
2. Daniel C. Roberts, "God of Our Fathers" (National Hymn), 1876.

I
THE NEW PAGANISM

WHEN CLARENCE DARROW, the notorious Atheist and equally notorious criminal Lawyer, stood before the judge and the jury and made his celebrated defense of young Leopold and Loeb, the brilliant but brutal murderers of the Franks boy, he said,

> "Your honor, if these boys are guilty, where did they get the philosophy which in their minds seems to justify their crime? Your honor, it does not meet with my ideas of justice to hang a nineteen-year-old boy for a philosophy of life which has been taught for the last twenty-five years in practically all the great Universities of this land."

This is a rather serious charge, and a charge concerning the truth or falsity of which every good citizen ought to be intelligent.

Historic Christianity has always been under fire. It always will be. But its enemies have never been more thoroughly organized and more determined in their assault than they are today.

12 *The New Paganism*

THE OLD PAGANISM AND THE NEW

The Old Paganism was content to train its artillery on the fundamental doctrines of Christianity. It lauded the Christian ideals of life but wholly repudiated the supernaturalism of its creed.

But the New Paganism has lifted its battle cry against the whole holy triumvirate of the Christian faith; its God, its creed, and its morality. It repudiates not only the distinctive doctrines of the Christian religion, but it makes blatant and blasphemous mockery of the holy ideals of conduct set up by Christianity as its standard of moral behaviour.

THIS IS THE ESSENTIAL DIFFERENCE BETWEEN THE OLD PAGANISM AND THE NEW.

John Stuart Mill, of the Old Paganism, said, "It would not be easy, even for the unbeliever, to find a better translation of the rule of virtue from the abstract into the concrete than to so live that Christ would approve our life."

Friederick W. Nietzsche, of the New Paganism, boasted that he had "torn the mask from Christian morality," and said of it, "It is the most malignant form of all falsehood that has ever corrupted mankind. It is the actual Circe of humanity."

Nietzsche has been followed by a whole brood of essayists, self-styled philosophers and university professors, like Samuel Schmalhausen, and Bertrand Russel, and so-called psychoanalytic physicians, like Sigmund Freud, and Alfred Adler, and Carl Jung and others of their ilk, as drastic in their strictures as the notorious Nietzsche himself. Then, we have others like Ben Linsey, H. G. Wells, Bernard Shaw, and Walter Lippman, who may express themselves a bit more mildly, but as plainly repudiate the ethical teachings of Christianity as they do the foundations upon which it rests.

And so it has come to pass that the literature of the day is saturated with pernicious teachings of the aforesaid sort. The market is flooded with books and booklets on Psychoanalysis, and Behaviourism, and Psychopathic Inferiority, and other phases of so-called Dynamic Psychology, many of which we regret to say are grossly godless and nauseatingly corrupt.

It will be interesting, therefore, and profitable as well, to investigate the charges made by Clarence Darrow, and see if our institutions of learning are to be held as largely responsible for it as some, in fact many, would have us believe.

The Case of Atheism

I. Unwelcome as the information is, it is folly to shut our eyes to the results of investigation such as has been made by the various questionnaires of recent years. Take, for instance, that now much exploited questionnaire by James H. Leuba, professor of psychology at Bryn Mawr College.

He questioned the students of nine of the leading Universities of the land and found that almost one-third of them, according to their own answers, deny the existence of a personal God and disbelieve also in personal immortality. The largest percentage of believers he found in the Freshman class and the smallest in the Senior class. To quote the professor,

> "The student statistics show that young people enter college with the beliefs still accepted in the average home of the land and that as their mental powers mature a large percentage of them abandon the cardinal Christian beliefs."

If this is true, then something of a rather serious nature is happening to our youth while they are in college. "It shows," says the Toronto Globe, "either a woeful lack of helpful direction for pliant minds or a deliberate effort to inoculate their minds with destructive germs."

In a second editorial he says,

> "It takes but slight familiarity with the teachings rife today in most of our college and university classrooms to have convincing proof that instructors and professors are constantly going out of their way to throw doubt or ridicule upon the teachings of the Bible with the result of shattering faith on the part of students."

This was said in response to an article that came out in the Varsity, the student publication of the University of Toronto, in the bold statement that Atheism is rampant in the university and that a majority of the students were "practical atheists." "This is not," says the Varsity, "an indictment on our part; it is a simple, straightforward statement of fact."

The University of Toronto forms no exception to the general situation today. Many of the students of our colleges and even of our High Schools are organized into Atheistic Clubs with definite programs for the propagation of their pernicious principles.

PROPAGANDA OF THE A.A.A.A.

These Clubs owe their origin very largely, if not altogether, to the American Association for the Advancement of Atheism, commonly known as the 4 A's. *The president of this American Association for the Advancement of Atheism is one Charles Smith, who boasts that he "persuaded his mother, a pious Methodist, to become an Atheist:"*

The 4 A's has taken for its slogan, its battle cry respecting Christianity, the American translation of Voltaire's "Ecrasez L'Infame," —KILL THE BEAST!!

In their published "Ten Demands" they demand among other things that we take "In God We Trust" from our coins; that the Bible be excluded from our public schools; that marriage be secularized with divorce upon request; that we stop running the Cross above the Flag; that Church property be taxed and all Chaplains be dismissed from public service, and so on with a number of other equally presumptuous, immoral and godless requests.

They began at once flooding the country with atheistic literature. High Schools and Colleges were circularized and Atheistic Clubs organized in many of our institutions of learning. I am told they are known by such titles as "The Damned Souls," "The Society of the Godless," and "The Legion of the Damned."

Wake Up, America!

Do we make a mistake when we sound a warning note against this increasing blasphemy? If the 18th century had its David Hume, the 20th has its John Dewey. If they had their Paine and their Voltaire, and later their Ingersol, we have our Menckens, our Smiths and our Darrows. *The situation is one about which we cannot afford to be indifferent.* History is replete enough with warning that comes out of the disastrous experience of nations where God has been denied or forgotten, and driven out of the nation's life.

We think of Russia where Atheism and Materialism are systematically taught in the schools; where churches are closed by order of the Soviet government; where store windows display atheistic decorations, and newspapers print daily cartoons ridiculing God and everything which decent people respect. But we need to contemplate with deep anxiety our own America where such things as those aforementioned are seemingly true, and where president Charles Smith has printed across the big front window of his office in Little Rock, Arkansas, "God is a ghost; the Bible is a lie." It is time for America to awake.

Now, we wonder if with the denial of God and the Christian Creed there does not follow naturally a denial of the

Christian standard of morals. So reasoned Nietzsche. To him
Christian ethics were as corrupt as its creed was foolish.

But anyhow, whether we owe it in any degree to
Nietzsche's philosophy or not, we are confronted today with
a very popular code of ethics which is an utter denial of the
Bible standard of holiness and an utter repudiation of the
pure and wholesome ideals of conduct which we have here-
tofore held dear as the only source of any real and abiding
peace for one's own soul, and as the only safeguard of the
security and happiness of our homes, or society and of our
national life.

THE CASE OF ETHICS

II. It would be interesting, as in the case of Atheism, to see
how far this sort of philosophy has found its way into our
institutions of learning and how far they are responsible
for inoculating the minds of our students with it.

The situation in many, and I fear in most of our larger
universities at least, can perhaps best be sensed by reading
something that comes from the desk of the president of
one of our state Universities. I refer to President Glenn
Frank, of the University of Wisconsin. Listen to this; he
says:

> "I suggest that young men trying to decide upon a pro-
> fession should read Bertrand Russell's "Education and
> the Good Life," for a vivid picture of the kind of edu-
> cation that seems to me worth fighting for, for the kind
> of education that able young men might well dedicate
> their lives to bringing about. It is an education that
> shall rescue sex from the slime of sentimentality and
> sniggering, and bring it into the sunlight of sincerity
> and sense."

Now what does Bertrand Russell have to say about
"rescuing sex" in this sublime volume which this noted
college president so warmly commends? Mr. Russell

may speak for himself. I quote:

"In teaching my own children I shall prevent them from learning a moral code which I regard as harmful. I shall not teach that faithfulness to one partner through life is in any way desirable, or that a permanent marriage should be regarded as excluding temporary episodes."

And this is the book that a college president commends to his students and to the youth of our land!!
But this, you say, is certainly an exceptional case! Would that it were so! But the fact is our country is flooded with literature foul enough to make Casanova blush with shame—books written very largely by college professors, recommended to the student body, copiously supplied by the college library, sold in the college bookstore and many of them used as text-books in the college classroom.

They claim to have discovered some new principle for redeeming life and making it *really* worth while. They call it the "New Psychology," and talk glibly of "Psychoanalysis" and "Behaviourism." Like Bertrand Russell they tell us that fidelity to the marriage vow belongs to an ethical code that is out of date. License before marriage they not only condone but actually recommend.

"Filthy Dreamers"

Questionnaires concerning such license, fit only for the minds of "filthy dreamers," are being put to your daughters and your sons by these advocates of the new educational standard in our colleges and universities. Witness the one put to the Senior Class in Smith College for young women, concerning which one indignant father said he felt like shooting the professor who perpetrated it. My regard for the reader's own sense of decency will not permit me to print for you questions 3, 10, 12, 16, 17, 18, and 19.

Of course, the literature referred to is not all equally outspoken, but it is all equally destructive of every worthy ideal of virtue and decency, and of the best interests of the individual, the family and the nation, while much of it is so vile we wonder how it escaped the censorship of the United States Mail.

Sigmund Freud[1] seems to have started the whole thing by his "Interpretation of Dreams." All dreams find their origin and their meaning in sex. Sex-repression is responsible for all our trouble.

Some of Freud's statements are so vile that we wonder how any mind other than one morally perverted could have produced them. The same thing is true of Schmalhausen's "Why We Misbehave," and Haverlock Ellis's "The Task of Social Hygiene," and Bertrand Russell's "Principles of Social Reconstruction," and Sherwood Anderson's "Dark Laughter," and John Ford's utterly nauseating narrative of Giovanni and Annabella, whose title no decent person cares to take upon his lips.

Concerning such books, and many others like them, The Baptist Witness, the official organ of more than 100,000 Baptists in the State of Florida, has said in an excellent editorial,

> "The wonder of it all is that men and women can be found in the teaching profession who would even handle such books, much less teach them. Well may we ask whither are we tending? If such matters are to be taught to our girls our civilization is doomed."

The young men and young women in our schools and colleges are soon to be our citizens, influencing our politics and making the laws that govern our country. What is to be the trend of our future policies in our homes, in society and in the life of our nation if those who are to make them have no belief in God, no belief in a hereafter, and that one is to gratify every desire of this life because it is the only

---

1. 1856-1939, still living when this book was written.

life there is, and the truly educated individual will get all he can out of it? WOULD YOU LIKE TO LIVE WHERE THIS SO-CALLED "NEW PSY-CHOLOGY" IS THE DOMINANT PHILOSOPHY OF LIFE? Would you like to rear your children in such an atmosphere? Do you think that public officials who take this philosophy of life as their ideal will, as a rule, stand the test when pressure is brought to bear upon them?

AMERICA'S GREATEST NEED

What we need in this country more than anything else is a great sweeping revival of religious faith. I mean the old-fashioned religion of our Fathers. No other has any power in it.

The New Paganism cannot last. We have found ourselves facing serious conditions before. But the Lord's arm was not shortened. Neither is it today.

They tell us that in 1872 in Princeton there were but two students who professed to be Christians, at Bowdoin in 1810 there was but one. The College Church at Yale in 1783 had but five members and when Lyman Beecher entered Yale as a student he found that most of the Senior class were infidels and called one another by such names as Voltaire, Tom Paine, Rousseau, D'Alembert, etc.

If this is true conditions were worse then than they are today. That is, so far as Atheism goes, but they were not sufficiently educated in those days to know anything about this "New Psychology" with its "libido" and its license, that esteems virtue lightly and would make a mockery of the holy ordinance of wedlock.

And yet in 1802 Yale experienced a revival of religion. One-third of the student body professed conversion and one-half of these became ministers. What happened at Yale happened at other colleges. At Williams in 1806 the famous Haystack Prayer-meeting took place where revival forces were born that moved the world. What happened in colleges happened everywhere. People turned again to God. Atheism was checked, the Church took on new life and power and the things of God became uppermost once more in the minds and lives of men.

I believe it may be so in our day.

There are those who say we are on the eve of some such great revival even now. But this I know—in spite of the atheistic tide in our universities; in spite of the poisonous psychoanalytic philosophy that threatens the very moral fiber of our youth; in spite of the present-day wide-spread unbelief, I know that in answer to agonizing prayer and earnest importunity we have a right to expect, and we ought to expect, a gracious outpouring of God's Spirit that will mean the shackles of doubt and of darkness broken and the bringing of our students and people in general by thousands and tens of thousands into the light and liberty of the glorious Gospel of our Lord and Saviour Jesus Christ.

Has He not said, "If my people which are called by my Name, shall humble themselves and pray and seek my face and turn from their sinful ways, THEN, will I hear from heaven and will forgive their sin and will heal their land."

WHERE IS THIS REVIVAL TO BEGIN? *I wish it might begin in me. It might, perhaps, begin in you, if you were willing.* IT MUST BEGIN WITH THE PEOPLE OF GOD.

II
THE MIRACLE OF THE MANGER

"Fear not to take unto thee Mary, thy wife, for that which is conceived in her is of the Holy Ghost. And she shall bring forth a son, and thou shalt call his name JESUS; for he shall save his people from their sins." — MATTHEW 1:20, 21.

THE MAN WHO DOES NOT BELIEVE IN THE STORY OF THE INCARNATION HAS NO CHRISTMAS TO CELEBRATE. Upon that story for 2,000 years the wisest and noblest characters of the world have found "the unmistakable marks of eternal truth," but for the Atheist, the Rationalist, the Infidel, who are bent on keeping all the stupendous facts of the Christian religion between the four walls of natural law, the miracle of the manger was only a human invention fabricated, as Elbert Hubbard declared, in the interest of a Jewish maiden's good name, and the Babe of Bethlehem a natural child born out of wedlock as the illegitimate offspring of a lecherous Jewish peasant.

A Beautiful Story

The story is as beautiful as it is familiar. joseph and Mary were normal lovers. Luke says Mary was "espoused" to Joseph. That means they were engaged. During the customary year which must elapse before marriage according to Judean law Joseph discovered that Mary, the girl he was to marry, was about to give birth to a child. Joseph was crushed. He felt he had been deceived and his honor injured, and he was much perplexed about what he ought to do. But he was a "just man," we are told, and he made up his mind to protect Mary and so far as possible not to let the public know anything about it. He would put her away quietly but he was "not willing to make a public example out of her." And while he thought on these things, deeply troubled in mind, an angel of the Lord came to him in a dream and said, "Joseph, fear not to take unto thee Mary, thy wife, for that which is conceived in her is of the Holy Ghost. And she shall bring forth a son, and thou shalt call his name Jesus; for he shall save his people from their sins."

The rest of the story runs quickly to its end: How Joseph made Mary his wife and how together they went down to Bethlehem to be taxed and while there the miracle of the manger took place.

And this is the story that some men refuse to believe. But denying the miracle of the manger only brings the unbelieving man up against a still harder proposition, namely, to account for Jesus Christ in some other way. The very person, the very character and career of Christ is the strongest argument for His miraculous birth.

No man ever lived such a wonderful life. his enemies watched Him like a hawk and the worst thing they could say about Him was that He did good on the Sabbath and that He let a sinful woman come close enough to Him to touch the hem of His garment.

No man ever uttered such wonderful teaching. It was so simple the common people heard Him gladly and yet so profound that no philosopher has ever been able to sound its depths. He never wrote a sermon. He never published a book. He never founded college to perpetuate His doctrines. And yet His teaching has endured for 2,000 years. It has been translated into every language under the sky and it has so transformed human life that whole nations have been lifted out of darkness and degradation by its power, and before this humble Galilean peasant the scholarship of the world uncovers its head today, and says, "Never man spake like this man."

And so I would like to ask the unbelieving man how he is going to account for Jesus Christ apart from the miracle of the manger. Isaiah said, "His name shall be called Wonderful." And there is no better name to describe Him.

He is the world's one great wonder.

He walked like a giant among the pigmies of the earth.

No one else ever approached Him.

He is in a class all by Himself.

He has no second.

If He was only a man, then by every law of progress and by every norm of reason this twentieth century ought to produce a better one.

Jesus Christ is the world's one great mystery, and the only clue you will find to His origin you will have to find in Luke 1:35 where it says, "The Holy Ghost shall come upon thee and the power of the Highest shall overshadow thee, and therefore that holy thing which shall be born of thee shall be called the Son of God."

What the Incarnation is

And now I am ready to tell you what the Miracle of the Manger really means. It means that when Jesus Christ came into this world He came into it with two natures—a human nature and a divine nature, and that this most extraordinary occurrence was brought about by the miraculous manner of His birth; that He was conceived by the Holy Ghost and born of a virgin mother.

AND THIS IS WHAT SOME PEOPLE REFUSE TO BELIEVE. They tell us the whole thing is an idea borrowed from pagan mythology. But this is only a "scarecrow," as another has said, "to frighten timid believers away from Christian truth just as gardeners try to frighten away the birds."

We know that the Greeks had a fable that Perseus was born of a virgin, Jupiter having come down to her in a shower of gold. And there is the Hindu myth of Krishna, born of the virgin Davaki through the direct power of their god. And there are doubtless others. But the similarity is only on the surface, and a mere cursory examination shows an impassable gulf between these heathen stories and the New Testament narrative.

Now, let us look at the record for a moment. It says that "When Mary was espoused to Joseph (that is, betrothed, engaged to him) she was found with child *before they came together.*"

IF JESUS WAS NOT CONCEIVED BY THE HOLY GHOST, THEN MARY WAS NOT A GOOD WOMAN, FOR JESUS WAS BORN OUT OF WEDLOCK. That is why the Jews called Him "the son of fornication." And this insult to His mother He resented as with flushed cheek and flashing eye He turned upon them and said, "Ye are of your father, the Devil."

LISTEN. IF JOSEPH WAS THE FATHER OF JESUS, WHY DID MARY SAY TO THE ANGEL, "HOW SHALL THIS THING BE, SEEING I KNOW NOT A MAN?"

IF JOSEPH WAS THE FATHER OF JESUS, WHY WAS HE MINDED TO PUT HER AWAY?

IF JOSEPH WAS THE FATHER OF JESUS, WHY DID GOD HAVE TO EXPLAIN TO HIM HOW IT ALL CAME ABOUT BEFORE HE WOULD TAKE HER BACK?

LISTEN. DID MARY ACT ANYTHING LIKE A GIRL WHO HAS GIVEN BIRTH TO AN ILLEGITIMATE CHILD? What a beautiful mystery the birth of a baby really is! Young womanhood's proudest moment is when that precious little life, *which is a very part of her own self, carried so long under her heart,* is laid for the first time upon her breast as heaven's sweetest and purest gift to virtue.

I like those tender and intensely human lines of Olga Petrova, entitled "To a Child that Enquires."

"How did you come to me, my sweet?
From the land that no man knows?
Did Mr. Stork bring you here on his wings?
Were you born in the heart of a rose?
Did an angel fly with you down from the sky?
Were you found in a gooseberry patch?
Did a fairy bring you from fairy-land
To my door—that was left on the latch?
No—my darling was born of a wonderful love,
A love that was daddy's and mine;
A love that was human, but deep and profound,
A love that was almost divine.
Do you remember, sweetheart, when we went to the
*   zoo?*
And we saw that big bear with a grouch?
And the tigers and lions, and that tall kangaroo
That carried her babes in a pouch?
Do you remember I told you she kept them there safe
From the cold and the wind till they grew
Big enough to take care of themselves
And dear heart, that's just how I first cared for you.
I carried you under my heart, my sweet,
And I sheltered you safe from alarms,
Till one wonderful day the dear God looked down
And my darling lay in my arms."

But the girl who is the mother of a child born out of wedlock can never be happy about it. She is ashamed and hangs her head in silent grief, and it is babies of this kind that are found so often on the doorstep of the orphanage or some rich woman's home.

But how did Mary act?

Was she embarrassed and did she hang her head in shame?

Did she sob?

NO, SHE SANG. She said, "My soul doth magnify the Lord!" She said, "Henceforth all generations shall call me blessed!"

Does that sound like a woman who is about to give birth to an illegitimate child? Does such a woman sing a Magnificat unto the Lord? Is it reasonable to believe that a young woman who is to become the mother of a child born out of wedlock would ever think of saying, "Henceforth all generations shall call me blessed"?

Once more. Mary went at once to her relatives. That's about the last place a girl in a trouble of the sort suggested would ever want to go. She would rather tell a stranger, for as a rule she would get less of criticism and more of sympathy.

But did Elizabeth criticise?

No. She called Mary "the mother of my Lord," and said, "Blessed art thou among women; and blessed is the fruit of thy womb!"

How is the unbelieving critic going to explain all this? Would Elizabeth, think you, have said such things to a young woman about to give birth to an illegitimate child? Let the destructive critics explain the actions of Joseph and Mary and Elizabeth psychologically, if they think they can; and if they can't, then let them hold their peace theologically.

And yet, some men refuse to believe. And Why?

1. YOU SAY YOU CAN'T UNDERSTAND IT. You can't understand how the human and the divine could combine to make a person out of Christ.

Well, can you understand how oxygen and hydrogen combine to make the water that you drink? Can you understand how oxygen and nitrogen combine to make the air that you breathe? Can you understand how body and soul combine to make a person out of you? You are a person, and if you can't understand the simpler union of matter and spirit that makes a person out of you, why do you stumble over the union of the divine and the human in the person of Christ? And please remember that transcending human reason is quite a different thing from contradicting it.

2. But you say the thing is so utterly impossible. It is contrary to all the laws of nature.

Well, let us not be too sure about these laws of nature. What about the female pheasants in the medical museum of the Royal College of Surgeons in London that were completely transformed into males. Had a woman certified that 2,000 years ago this unbelieving world would be saying today, "Preposterous, Violation of natural law, Impossible!"

The scientific name for virgin birth is Parthenogenesis, and it is a recognized fact today in some of the lower forms of life, such as the silkworm, the honey bee, sawflies and beetles, where occasional cases of birth without a male parent have been noted. And if science, by a simple operation, can render this thing possible in the lower realm of life, I wonder just how foolish a man would be to believe that God could not do it in the higher.

But why argue the matter? Nothing is impossible with God. Some people are awfully afraid of the supernatural. If you admit one miracle you might as well admit them all. What kind of a God do you want us to worship? A God who can't do this and can't do that and can't do the other? I believe in a God who can do anything. Why not?

3. Well, you say, If the story is true, why are there not

MORE WITNESSES TO IT IN THE BIBLE? But how many witnesses does God require to prove His Word? It was recorded by the prophets at least 800 years before the son of Mary was born. It was recorded by two of the evangelists after He was born. It is supported by the question of Mary, and by her conduct as well as that of Joseph and Elizabeth. And all this in language so plain that a child can read and not misunderstand.

I know that some of the New Testament writers say nothing about it, and the unbelieving critic claims that their silence implies denial. But one can just as well say that their silence implies their acceptance of it, for if they knew about it, as they must have known, and knew it was not true they most assuredly would have been under obligation to Almighty God and to man to say so.

If silence implies denial, then by that rule of logic the authenticity and the truthfulness of almost every statement found in the New Testament concerning Jesus can be destroyed.

John says nothing about the Transfiguration. THEREFORE THERE WAS NO TRANSFIGURATION! Yet Matthew, Mark, and Luke say John was one of the three disciples who was there.

Matthew, Mark and Luke say nothing about the resurrection of Lazarus. THEREFORE LAZARUS WAS NEVER RAISED FROM THE DEAD!

Mark and John say nothing about the birth of Jesus. THEREFORE HE WAS NEVER EVEN BORN! These two Gospels, for reasons quite pertinent, begin with His public ministry, and so had no occasion to mention His birth. But both of them specifically call Him the Son of God, and John repeatedly calls Him the Only Begotten Son of God.

What does "begotten" mean? It means to generate, to bring into existence. Did John mean that Jesus was begotten of Joseph, or did he mean what he said, namely, that He was the ONLY BEGOTTEN SON OF GOD?

Was Jesus the son of Joseph?

The prophets say, "No."
Matthew says, "No."
Mark says, "No."
Luke says, "No."
John says, "No."
Joseph says, "No."
Mary says, "No."
Elizabeth says, "No."
The Angel says, "No."
Christ says, "No."
God says, "No."
The Modernist says, "Yes."

And all I can say is — I cannot understand how in the face of such overwhelming testimony any man could be willing to prostitute his brain and his soul either by mutilating the Word of God or insulting the mother of Jesus in this Satan-inspired but futile endeavor to snatch from the brow of Jesus Christ this piece of the incontrovertible evidence of His glorious Godhood.

"The Word was made flesh and dwelt among men." How we thank God that Jesus came! He might have come some other way, but what it could have been is beyond the knowledge of man to conceive, but the human mind can think of no more beautiful way, no more reasonable way, no more fitting way He could have come than by the way He did come — the way of His supernatural Virgin Birth.

I hear some one say, "But after all it makes no difference *how* He came."

BUT IT DOES MAKE A DIFFERENCE. Let the attack upon the Cradle go unchallenged and they will train their attack upon His Cross. Let them deny the miracle of His Birth and they will next deny the miracle of His Resurrection, of His Ascension, and of His Return and we will be without any Christ at all.

IT DOES MAKE A DIFFERENCE.

IF JESUS HAD A HUMAN FATHER, then the Bible is not true.

IF JESUS HAD A HUMAN FATHER, then He was not pre-existent from all eternity and was only a human being.

IF JESUS HAD A HUMAN FATHER, then He had a sinful nature, as all men have, and instead of being the Saviour of others He would have needed a Saviour for Himself.

IF JESUS HAD A HUMAN FATHER, then there was no redemptive value to His death on the Cross.

IF JESUS HAD A HUMAN FATHER, then when they took His life He would have had no power to "take it up again" in the Resurrection; no power to ascend to His Father; no power to come again in the clouds with the angels and the great glory.

Hear me, oh men and women, as I say to you that it was none other than the Spirit of the Almighty God Himself, the Eternal Father, functioning through His own direct and immediate generative power that constituted the Son of Mary the sinless, Sovereign Saviour of the world.

If you have ever said it before, don't, I plead with you, ever say it again, in thoughtless indifference, that it makes no difference whether Jesus had or did not have a human father. If Jesus was not born as the record says He was, then He was not the Son of God, and there was no Emmanuel, "God with Us"; no "Lamb of God that taketh away the sin of the world," and we are yet in our sins, without God; without any assurance of immortality or without any hope of heaven.

THE PURPOSE OF THE INCARNATION

But I am not so much concerned, and I am sure you are not, about HOW the Miracle of the Manger took place, as I am about WHY it ever took place at all; why God ever made that Christmas night bright with the Star that shone above the little city of His birth.

HE DID IT FOR THREE REASONS.

1. *In First John 3:5 we are told that He came to take away sin.*

THAT MEANS PARDON FOR THE PAST.

Isn't that a bit of the most glorious news you ever heard! I tell you, to the man whose soul is lashed with the whips of a guilty conscience, to the man who knows his sin and hates the memory of it, the sweetest story ever told, the sweetest song ever sung, the sweetest message ever delivered is the glad news that in some mysterious way that he can never fully understand the Man of the Manger puts Himself down underneath the sin and the shame and all the unholy past of his life, and, lifting it up and off from his soul, bears it forever away. And yet that is what He came to do.

2. *Then, in First John 3:8 we are told that He came to destroy the works of the Devil.*

THAT MEANS HELP FOR THE PRESENT.

The only thing that I'm afraid of in all the universe of God is sin. That is the work of the Devil. My brother, if you must play with something dangerous, go out into the field and play with a rattler; go down to the electric road and play with the third rail; reach up into the skies and play with the forked lightning, but for God's sake, as you value your soul, do not play with sin.

But thank God, sin never took any man so far down but that Christ Jesus, the God-Man, could reach that far down, and farther, and snap the fetters and set him free.

3. *And once more, in John 10:10 we are told that He came that you and I might have life, and have it more abundantly —eternal life, here and now and forever.*

THAT MEANS HOPE FOR THE FUTURE.

What a value that places on your soul and mine in the sight of God! "How much then is a man better than a sheep!" said Jesus one day in exclamation. Yes, how much better!

God would never have sent His Son into this world; He would never have made this dark earth bright with the shining Star of Bethlehem for all the gold and diamonds its mines could ever yield; no, not for all the sheep on ten thousand hills, but He did it for you and for me. And if your soul and mine are of such infinite value in His sight ought they not to be the thing of supreme value in our own? What an act, therefore, of the greatest folly to neglect its salvation! "For what shall it profit a man if he gain the whole world and lose his own soul?"

And here is the invitation: "The Spirit and the bride say, 'Come.' And let him that is athirst come; and whosoever will let him take of the water of life freely."

> *"I can but perish if I go;*
> *I am resolved to try;*
> *For if I stay away, I know*
> *I shall forever die."*

III
CHRIST AND THE DOMESTIC WORLD

"What have they seen in thy Home?" —II KINGS 20:15

THE LOVELIEST WORD in all the myriad languages of the world is the word "Home."

On the tenth day of April, 1852, an American citizen died in Algiers. They laid him to sleep in a little cemetery at Tunis, the capital city, and there they let him lie for thirty-one years until America's sense of honor came back and we sent a United States man-o'-war to bring him back to his native land. They digged up his body, placed it on board the vessel and headed for the homeland.

As the vessel drew near bands of music went out to greet it; the big guns thundered out their welcome from the forts, and all the flags hung at half-mast to do honor to his memory. A special train bore his remains to Washington. Business was suspended in the halls of Congress and in the store. The President and his cabinet, members of congress, officers of the army and navy stood with uncovered head as the funeral procession moved along Pennsylvania avenue. The rich and the poor were there, the mighty and the humble all bowed in reverence for the man whose ashes were carried by.

33

Who was the man?

What great battle had he fought? None.

What great book had he written? None.

What great oration had he delivered? None.

What great painting had he spread on canvas? None.

What great invention had he perfected? None.

What great engineering feat had he accomplished?
None.

What had he done?

He had written a song; a song sung by the millionaire in
his mansion, by the sons of toil in the factory and the field,
and by the soldiers in the trench; a song sung by the rich
and poor alike. The man in the coffin was John Howard
Payne, and the song he had written was,

> *"Home, sweet, sweet, home;*
> *Be it ever so humble,*
> *There's no place like home."*

WHAT A MAGIC WORD IT IS! As you listen to its sound you
are no longer here in this audience, but you have gone with
a flight swifter than the glance of a sparkling star, some of
you back to the green hills of Pennsylvania, some of you
to the whispering pines of Maine, some to the rolling plains
of the middle-west, and some of you across the waters that
roll between other lands and this one we call our own, back,
back to the place of all places the dearest and best—the
place you called your home;

> *"the spot of earth supremely blest,*
> *a dearer, sweeter spot than all the rest."*

What is Home? Well, it is not a house.

> *"A house is built of bricks and stones, of sills and*
> *posts and piers;*
> *But a home is built of loving deeds that stand a*
> *thousand years.*

*A house, though but a humble cot, within its walls
    may hold
A home of priceless beauty, rich in love's eternal
    gold."*

YOU CAN PILE UP GRANDEUR AND MISS THE SOUL OF A THING.
You can fill the mansion you build with magnificence of
every kind and find out through bitter experience that it
has no heart. I wonder how much of the real home there is
in some of the palatial residences that adorn many of the
boulevards. Some of the saddest hearts in God's world move
about in the midst of luxury and beauty.

I have been a guest in many such a place both here
and elsewhere. I have admired the hand-painted ceil-
ings and the masterpieces of art upon the walls—copies
from Rubens, Raphael, Rembrandt, Murillo, and
Reynolds, and sometimes the original. I have feasted my
eyes upon the snowy statuary—marble from Carrara,
from Paros, and from Mount Pentelicus. I have gazed
upon the handsome furniture — mahogany, bird's-eye
maple, and Circassian walnut. I have seen the sideboard
groan beneath the weight of cut-glass and hand-painted
china. And I have stood with my feet sinking in the soft
Oriental rugs and said, "All this you may have, and
more; your cook may be a high-salaried chef from Paris
and the choicest food may adorn your tables; you may
recline on silken cushions and ride in a faultless limou-
sine, but if love is not there and the kindly graces flow-
ing from it that make the home what it really ought to
be, the place you imagined to be a home will become a
mausoleum full of dead hopes and dead expectations
and dead ideals and the handsome furnishings will be
like skeletons of other days to mock you with the
thought of what might have been.

THE HOME IS THE HEART OF CIVILIZATION. A wise teacher of
the ancient world said, "Give me a single domestic grace

and I will turn it into a hundred public virtues." It is like a great reservoir pouring its waters through every avenue of moral, social and political life.

Those waters may be healing or they may be hurtful, according to the character of the Home, and it takes no exceptional wisdom to declare that the life of the community, and indeed the life of the nation, will never rise any higher nor fall an lower than the life of the home.

AMERICAN LIFE IN A BAD WAY

Nor does it take any particular wisdom to see that American life is in a bad way and sadly in need of some tonic for its moral and spiritual invigoration.

Look at the crime-wave that has been sweeping over the land, the bold and daring methods of daylight robbery, and the curse of strong drink coming upon us again. Sabbath breaking is appalling. Social immorality is holding high carnival. Marriage is a plaything. Atheism stalks abroad with impudent, defying air and Communism threatens to turn our country red. *If ever there was a day when the American nation needed moral and spiritual reinforcement from some quarter surely that day is with us now.*

What is to be done about it? You say, "Enforce the law." Yes, that ought to be done. But you can't reform society with a club. Reformation produced that way is about as enduring as "permanent waves." You've got to deal with the thing that enters into the making of society. And while there are other influences to be reckoned with I know of no influence that has quite so much to do with the thing we are talking about as that which is brought to bear upon the children in the home, and we shall never save the youth of this nation nor the nation itself from any of the evils that threaten its life until we push the battle across the threshold of the American home.

When I speak of Christ and the domestic world I am not referring to Christ's example in the home, for of this Scripture tells us practically nothing, but I have in mind the characteristics of a home where due regard obtains for the principles of Christ and where the affairs of home-life are regulated as He would regulate them if it were His privilege as it is His right to do so. And concerning this home there are a number of things that may be said with propriety and with profit.

Importance of Parental Authority

1. The Christian Home is a place where Children are taught respect for parental authority. Lawlessness in the nation gets its start at the fireside of the American home. A child that has not respect for the authority of its parents will have no respect for the authority of God, nor the powers that be when he comes to maturity.

Many a child is ruined by the over-indulgence of a pair of easy-going parents. A mother who raised seven noble sons without a black sheep among them was asked how she did it. She replied, "I did it with prayer and hickory." I like the prayer, but "I hae me doots" about the hickory, and yet I remember that God said of Abraham, "I know Abraham—that he will command his children after him, and they shall keep the way of the Lord."

Christian Example

2. The Christian Home is a place where due consideration is given to the importance of Christian example and influence.

More time will be spent together in the family circle. Too many so-called homes are mere lunch-counters with lodging quarters attached. Many a child does not have a real fair chance to get well acquainted with its parents. If parental influence means anything it needs time to do its work.

The cuckoo, I am told, is too indolent to build her own nest. She goes around and lays her eggs in the nest of Mr. and Mrs. Sparrow and they have to hatch the egg and feed that everlasting cuckoo while Mr. and Mrs. Cuckoo are busy gadding about and discharging their social obligations, whatever that may mean. Perhaps the cuckoo doesn't know any better, but surely the mother who so far fails to appreciate not alone the obligation, but the mighty and ever persistent fact of parental influence upon character as to leave her children to the tender mercies of the nurse, the maid, and the governess while she busies herself continually with affairs outside the home, of whatever nature they may be, is a matter of regret deplorable beyond the power of words to express.

Who can estimate the influence of home-life upon character! Live in a court and you will become courtly; live with wolves and you will learn to howl.

In a test case of 120 clergymen 100 of them assigned the means of their conversion to the influence of Christian homes, and in another instance where 374 came into fellowship with the Church on confession of faith 327 of them made the same claim for the homes in which they were reared. But Tom Paine said, "I was an infidel before I was five years old."

They tell us that over in the lovely island of Sicily when the sun rises, the shadow of Mt. Etna is cast far across the land, resting on the gardens, the groves, the fields and the homes of the people. And it is always a shadow of gloom, as everybody knows, a shadow that speaks of an ever imminent terror. And just like that is the shadow of ungodly parental influence that hangs over the life of a child to the very close of its earthly career.

A little fellow who was asked by his Sunday School teacher, "Who made you?" gave at once a most theological and practical answer. He said, "God made me and I growed the rest." *But you might as well expect flowers to grow underneath the snows of the Klondike as to expect a holy character to grow in the midst of the atmosphere furnished, alas, by too many of our homes today.*

You know the lobster swims backwards and this greatly annoyed a certain number of fish, and so they proposed forming a class of instruction for the young lobsters, gravely arguing that if they commenced young as they grew up they would learn to swim correctly. A number of young lobsters came and did exceedingly well in moving forwards, but when they returned home and saw their fathers and mothers swimming in the old way they soon forgot all they had learned and were at it too. And when those to whom God has entrusted the making of the home learn that it is not so much by restrictive measures; not so much by rigid, Draconian "Thou shalt nots," not so much by good advice, but by their own example, their own lives, creating thereby an atmosphere instinct with holy thoughts and pure ideals and noble inspirations they will find the blessing of God resting upon an unbroken family circle, the bud and the blossom, of which heaven itself will one day be the fruit.

Family Worship

3. The Christian Home is a place where together the Word of God is read and prayer is made for His blessing on the family.

Can you recall that beautiful picture in "The Cotter's Saturday Night," by Bobbie Burns, where the family in the evening gathers round the open hearth and "the priest-like father reads the sacred page," and then kneeling down to heaven's Eternal King "the saint, the patriot and the father prays." That is what I mean.

Religion was a thing of the home long before it became an affair of the Church. Our first parents were priests. God Himself ordained them to holy orders. And because of this primal consecration God expects every man to be a priest in his own household.

If God has made any duty plain in His Word it is this one. Listen: "And these words which I command thee this

day shall be in thy heart, and thou shalt teach them dili-
gently unto thy children. Thou shalt talk of them when
thou sittest in thine house, and when thou liest down and
when thou risest up." How could a man expect to fulfill
a word like that and be the head of a home where God
is forgotten and His Word neglected and where the children are reared without the sound of song or prayer to
hallow the atmosphere with an influence that makes for
things eternal?

There is nothing that so hallows, so glorifies and so sweet-
ens the home-life as this beautiful custom. It makes the
home like Tom Moore's vase—perfumed by the roses it
carries. It strengthens the soul for life's duties; it removes
all friction and softens the heart with a forgiving spirit; "It
weaves into the fabric of memory," as another has said,
"silver threads that remain bright and shining forever." It
binds with golden chains about the feet of God, and though
many a son and daughter has wandered away in spite of it
all, when years have gone and the home voices have grown
silent and the old homestead perhaps has become the property of others, the memory of those praying hours has
brought many a prodigal back in tears to the God of their
childhood days.

What Love Can Do

4. And then best of all the Christian Home is a place
where love is the ruling virtue—where Love comes to its
own and fills every relationship with its own sweet spirit.

Father, when you come home in the evening what does
your coming mean to the family? A child hearing of heaven
and being told his father would be there replied, "Oh, then
I dinna want to gang."

You know it is said that in every Christian home there
are two bears. One is Bear and the other is Forbear, the
"two words of household peace."

It has been said that "home is the only spot on earth

where the faults and the failings of fallen humanity are hidden under the mantle of charity?" But, "Alas for the rarity of Christian charity" in many a home.

And what half, and sometimes whole, tragedies do these words suggest—homes that began with bright promise of sweetness coming with the years but are now transformed into bleak and wintry places where hearts grow numb and the twain who became one in love's holiest moment are twain in heart once more.

Maria and David were driving along. The team was pulling a heavy load and when they came to a hard place they settled down in the harness and pulled together.

"David," said Maria, "why can't we pull together like that?"

"We could," replied David, "if like that team there was only one tongue between us."

But love can make one tongue out of two. I mean, the rather, it can make two tongues to talk like one. No matter what happens in the home or anywhere else,

"*Love can split the sky in two,*
And make the face of God shine through."

There is a heroism about real forbearance finer than the taking of a city. Sinclair Lewis devoted several hundred pages in "Main Street" to an attempt to make a heroine out of Carol Kenniscott, but I really think the real hero of the tale was Dr. Will Kenniscott, whom the author rather shamefully neglected, but who refused to distress himself because of the unreasonable annoyance of an inconsiderate wife.

Yes, forbearance is a splendid virtue, and we need to remember with Cowper,

"*The kindest and the happiest pair,*
Will find occasion to forbear;
Find something every day they live,
To pity, and perhaps forgive."

But even better than forbearing is the virtue of bearing —
the going out of the heart in self-forgetful ministry, the
ministry that is born of love. I do not mean so much the
ministry to material wants—for this always follows—but
the thoughtfulness that seeks to make provision for the
wants of one's deeper nature. You have spoken few unkind
words in your home, but have you spoken very many kind
ones? Is your home like the preacher's in George Eliot's
story? Is it like the home of Jane Carlyle, which, alas, was
no creation of the novelist but a tragic reality where, as
one suggests, "the man never told her that he loved her—
but once, and that was an exaggeration." "What about
those little tokens of affection that make home for both so
radiant and so bright? Just how large is the place your mate
really holds in your affection and your consideration?

I wonder if you are anything like the man who dashed
into the police station at midnight, explaining that his wife
had been missing since eight o'clock that morning, and
asking that search be made for her.

"Her description," said the sergeant. "Height?"

"I—I don't know!"

"Weight?"

The husband shook his head vaguely.

"Color of eyes?"

"Just average, I think."

"Do you know how she was dressed?"

"I expect she wore her coat and hat. She took the dog
with her."

"What kind of a dog?"

"Brindle bull-terrier, weight fourteen and a half pounds,
four dark blotches on his body, shading from grey to white.
Round, blackish spot over the left eye, white stub tail, three
white legs and right front leg brindled, all but the toes. A
small nick in the left ear, a silver link collar, with—."

"That'll do!" gasped the sergeant; "we'll find the dog."

The blind Bishop in Victor Hugo's "Les Miserables" called

his home "a paradise of darkness," because he had his sister by his side and he "possessed her entire heart."

Oh, for a love in the home like that. And only Christ can bring it. And when love like that is in every home we will no longer need the sanctuary of God, for our homes will be our churches and earth will become a paradise prepared for the coming of the New Jerusalem wherein dwelleth righteousness.

May God bless your home. May it be a place where the fine, sweet influence of Christ shall make rich the atmosphere with the aroma that comes from all that is highest and holiest in human relationship, and when you have gone down one by one through the shadow of death's dark valley may it be your glorious heritage to meet again in an unbroken family circle on the flower-grown banks of love's pure river and be at home with Christ forever in the Father's house on high.

IV
CHRIST AND THE SOCIAL WORLD

"Ye are the light of the world. Neither do men light a candle and put it under a bushel, but on a candlestick and it giveth light unto all that are in the house."

ARISTOTLE CALLED MAN a political animal. In a sense, Yes; but he is par excellence a social animal. Man is gregarious. The fowls of the air in flocks, the beasts of the field in herds, the fish in schools, and man in society—this is the divine arrangement.

"Oh for a lodge in some vast wilderness," sounds well enough in verse, but human beings in general are not looking for Robinson Crusoe experiences. Once in a while we come across some unsocial, unapproachable individual whose peculiar but non-Christian conception of sainthood has made him a self-ostracized recluse, a Simon Stylites, sitting forever on his lonely pillar, a Noe Sanchez Martin walking 18 kilometers with 154 nails with points up in his shoes, performing his vows to the Black Madonna, each one a world unto himself. But there is something in most of us, an instinct that craves the society of others, and makes us all the happier because of it. And God wants His people happy.

The idea that when a man becomes a Christian he must "hang his harp on a weeping willow tree," and bid solemn adieu to the frolicking gladness and exuberance of life is a slander on what Christianity really is. I know that Solomon said, "Vanitas vanitatum; omnia est vanitas," Vanity of vanities; all is vanity, but I think he must have said that when his 700 wives were pestering the life out of him, and I prefer the old man's mood when in another place describing religion, he said, "Her ways are ways of pleasantness and her paths are paths of peace."

The pleasures of society are one of the birthrights of God's people. Jesus was Himself very much of a society man. I simply mean by that, He mingled much with His fellowmen. He began His ministry by attending a wedding. He was the guest of all classes. He accepted their hospitality and dined at their tables. It was because of this that the false-hearted and narrow-souled critics of His day called Him a glutton and a wine-bibber.

But Jesus never went into any man's home nor into any circle of society but that He left upon it the impress of His holy influence. "Ye are the light of the world," but a candle is not supposed to shine under a bushel measure. "Ye are the salt of the earth." A little fellow, in reply to the teacher's question, said, "Salt is the thing that makes your potatoes taste bad when you don't put any in." And salt barreled up in the Church will never season an unsavory world.

Christianity is not a thing of cathedrals and prayer meetings. It is God's indispensable requisite for the highest and best in every sphere of life—for the rushing, straining life of business, the tempting, trying life of politics, the anxious, earnest life of the home, and the laughing, lighthearted life of society. And the Christian is not supposed to be some delicate novelty housed up in a glass case, that will go all to pieces if it comes in contact with the hard world. He is not supposed to be a hot-house plant, but a plant with a capacity for becoming a sturdy oak that can brave the threatening storms; a living, walking dynamo, if you please, charging and changing the world with the magnetic influence of an unseen power that comes from a source to which a man without the grace of Christ in his heart is an utter stranger.

Suppose that all whose lives stand for the teachings of Jesus should suddenly withdraw from society—that society be given over entirely to those who know nothing about the impulse nor the restraint that characterizes the life of every true child of God! Then let some Ward McAllister take his pen after awhile and write again for us, "Society as I have Found it," and what sort of a story do you think it would be? I don't know where you would find a better answer, so far as the bon-ton and Elite folks are concerned, than in the so-called best society of Nero's day so graphically depicted for us in the justly celebrated story entitled "Quo Vadis?"

THE LIGHT UNDER A BUSHEL

The great thing to be deplored today is that so many Christians who go into society fail to take their Christianity with them as they go. I mean, of course, Christians so-called. They hide their light under a bushel instead of letting it shine for Christ.

There comes to my mind the story of a fashionable young woman who was really an exceptional Christian. Her strict adherence on all occasions to what she believed was right made it a bit unpleasant for her at times. She was invited to spend the week-end in connection with a rather prominent social event and thought within herself that for once she would be very careful not to make herself noticeable in any way because of any religious scruples she might have.

It worked very well, but on the closing evening a somewhat fashionable and worldly woman asked her to stroll with her and said to her:

"Where is your sister? Why did she not come? I mean the one who is known as 'the religious Miss J.?' I have gotten so tired of the empty and unworthy pleasures and excitements of this world that I have just longed to have a talk with a real Christian. It was because I thought your sister was coming that I accepted the invitation and I am so sorry she is not here."

With deep embarrassment and in tears which she could not restrain, she confessed that she had no sister and that she was the one they called the "religious Miss J." but that shame for the badge she should have so gladly and so proudly worn had caused her not to let it be known.

Drawing Room Evangelism

Contrast with that the beautiful consistency of the wife of General McAlpin, remembering in the drawing room, as everywhere else, the purpose for which she had been set in the world. She was at one time one of the gayest of New York City's social set, but after her conversion she went to Albany to uphold the social dignity of her husband's position. General McAlpin had been appointed a member of Governor Morton's staff. At the Governor's reception Mrs. McAlpin inaugurated what in that day became known as "Drawing Room Evangelism" by talking to the Governor's two daughters about the joy she had in serving Christ.

If the people in Palm Beach society who call themselves Christians, who profess the name of Jesus, would but remember the opportunity and the responsibility which is theirs what an elevation of the moral tone of Palm Beach society it would really mean!

It would mean an elevation of that tone which would manifest itself in a number of ways, a few of which I now want to mention.

I. THERE WOULD BE LESS OF SHAM IN SOCIETY. Less of tom-foolery. Don't forget that humanity has a far greater genius for what is natural than for what is affected.

The world's so-called "high society" is full of feather-brained fops who have only ambition enough and animation enough to glide across the parlor floor with sickly dignity to pick up a lady's fan.

This kind of society is like a large piece of frozen water where skating well is considered the greatest accomplishment, cutting those graceful curves of Chesterfieldian polish, and giving consideration to a score of other senseless infinitesimals that call for a course in social art in order to become a star of fashionable perfection.

But that's about all you can expect as long as the test of worthiness is the kid glove and the latest bow instead of the adornment of a manly spirit and a humble heart.

When real worth comes to its own in society and nothing but Christian influence can bring it about—society will rid itself also of the social hypocrite. I mean the bowing, smiling guest under whose immaculate shirt-front is often found a maculate heart—black underneath the white—and who, were the mask torn away, would be discovered a polite knave and a well-dressed libertine.

We do not tolerate a man in society with an unclean face, but what about the man with an unclean heart. For my own part I prefer that kind of heathenism which, as Bishop Potter once said, "wallows in filth and disgusts the beholder" rather than that heathenism which covers up its walking putrefaction with the latest creations of fashion and rides in liveried turnouts with rosetted flunkies to wait upon its every whim. "We have been talking so much," said the Bishop, "about the Gospel for the masses; now let us talk a little about the Gospel for the lepers of society, for the portable lazarettoes of upper-tendom."

II. There would be less of social caste in society.

It is said of Lowell, "He died in the war; and he danced with the girls with whom others did not care to dance." I call attention neither to his patriotism nor to his dancing, but to that true gentlemanly courtesy which constitutes the knighthood of the New Chivalry, and stands for the eternal condemnation of this "better-than thou-ism" which is contemptible and unchristian in society as it is everywhere else.

"A Man's a Man for a' That"

They were talking about a certain young man—a couple ladies of the upper circle; he was far above the average in intelligence, and his character was irreproachable, "But," said one of the ladies, "he wouldn't shine very much in a New York parlor," and the verdict was unanimous. It seemingly takes a Stanford White to shine there.

It has ever been thus and we need in this day as much as ever in the midst of the narrow, pharisaical barriers intersecting society, to remember what we read in the lines of Bobby Burns, that all too often, "The rank is but the guinea's stamp," and

"What tho' on hamely fare we dine,
    Wear hodden. gray, an' a' that;
Gie fools their silks, and knaves their wine—
    A man's a man for a' that!
For a' that, an' a' that,
    Their tinsel show, an' a' that;
The honest man, though e'er sae poor,
    Is king o' men for a' that!"

III. There will be less of extravagance in society.

Certainly it is unchristian to live beyond your means. Because your neighbor has Persian rugs is no reason why you should not be satisfied with Brussels carpet. Benedict Arnold sold his country to pay his wife's society bills.

The great sin of extravagance lies in its practical denial of responsibility. It is hardly to be wondered at that the poor are sometimes incensed against the rich as long as there are single banquets in this land costing almost a fortune to provide them, and when the wife of one of our ambassadors appears in a foreign court with $250,000.00 worth of diamonds sparkling on her bosom, and when a whole square of disease-breeding tenements could be demolished and others of decent plumbing and ventilation erected for the price of a lady's wardrobe.

COURTING COMMUNISM

I saw an account of a dog party the other day that made me smile a bit. It was given in Hotel Vanderbilt and the list of guests in the New York papers ran like this: Mrs. Carl E. Holliday and dog; Mrs. William Cline and dog; Miss Gertrude Ashley and dog; Mrs. Reginald Brittian and dog. It reminded me of an epitaph I saw on a marble stone in a dog graveyard:

PRINCE
Dearly Beloved
Born May 4, 1882—Died November 9, 1897
"And of such is the kingdom of heaven"

Now I like dogs. I think there is something wrong with a woman or a man who does not love a dog. But what shall we say of a dog party given in Hyde Park some time ago where the pugs and the poodles and the Pekinese wore seal-skin covers and diamonds in their ears, and were fed on beefsteak at seventy-five cents a pound, while just around the corner starving babies were crying for milk and were put to bed hungry because there was no bread? *Some ladies can cry over a thing like that and wipe away their tears with a fifty-dollar handkerchief.*

Some people seek to justify the extravagances of modern society with the plea that such methods of living furnish just that much more employment for the poor. If men were misers and buried their gold that might be true, but for the man who appreciates, even in the slightest degree, the responsibility that comes with wealth such an argument is deserving of very little consideration indeed. It reminds one of those homely lines, the author of which I do not know:

"Now Dives daily feasted and was gorgeously ar
    rayed,
Not at all because he liked it, but because 'twas
    good for trade;
That the people might have calico, he clothed himself
    in silk,
And surfeited himself with cream that they might
    have more milk.
He fed five hundred servants that the poor might not
    lack bread,
And has his vessels made of gold that they might
    have more lead;
And e'en to show his sympathy with the deserving
    poor,
He did no useful work himself that they might do
    the more."

IV. There will be less of the questionable in society. Less of gilded immorality.

Because a man is a clergyman he is not, therefore, ipse facto [sic], a joy-killer. But there is much — very much, indeed, — about the social doings of these days that cannot be condemned too unsparingly, and the faithful minister will not fail to lift his voice against it.

Of course, no one, I hardly suppose the participants themselves, would have a word to say in defense of the wild, and debauching orgies in which many of the swell social affairs end — parties like a certain one described by a Japanese servant who said, "I served the cocktails, the highballs and the wine; green drinks, yellow drinks, and purple. One of the guests threw a plate of food at me. They thought it was fun and soon the food was flying all over the room. Costly china plates smashed against the wall, decanters crashed through mirrors, and whiskey and wine were dashed into each other's face. They whooped and laughed and yelled." And other things the servant described it will not do to mention here.

I have been told that social doings of this sort are not altogether foreign to Palm Beach. I do not know. You know the tragic suicide of Margaret Harding was charged by her father against the social whirl of the nation's capital, and the investigation that followed furnished any amount of evidence that "smart society" was honeycombed with recklessness, secret debauchery, shameless exposure of nudity, drinking of all kinds of intoxicants, and other vices unfit to be mentioned. And what is true of the nation's capital is pretty generally true throughout the land in that particular kind of society.

The fault lies, I fear, in the countenance given, even by all too many professing Christians, to the things that lead to such debauchery. I mean the things that Paul calls "inexpedient," the questionable things of society, the things which Paul says "do not edify," but on the contrary rob us of all spiritual strength and beauty and of the influence that ought to bless and not to blight the lives of others with whom we mingle in the social world or other spheres of life.

CHRIST CROWDED OUT

If Christ were given His rightful place in your life, the place of supremacy which is really His, and you were to settle all matters of questionable indulgence by giving an honest answer to the question, "What Would Jesus Do?" you would be walking in a path of light and peace and like Jacob of old you would "have power with God and with man," and you would be a blessing to society, and not, perhaps, the hurtful influence you are today. I wonder if I would make a mistake were I to say that Christ held that place, a bit more largely at least, in the lives of some of you before you came to Palm Beach. Does wintering in Palm Beach make a difference?

I have a friend who says, "I can never forget my first sight of a painting by Paul Veronese, 'The Marriage at Cana,' in the *Salle Carre* of the Louvre in Paris. It has all that marvelous mellow richness which characterizes the Venetian School. The composition is equally wonderful. Eleanor of Austria, Queen of France, is there. Francis the First is there. Mary of England is there. The Sultan Solyman is there. The Emperor Charles is there. It is a scene of pomp and splendor such as we read of occasionally in the pages of history.

"After looking at it for a time it suddenly occurred to me to ask, 'How about the Christ?' He is the man with the artificial halo about His head. Take that halo from the picture, and you would scarcely know that he was there, buried as He is under all this magnificence. He is not remarkable, as in some paintings, for the light of love that shines in His eyes. He is distinguished simply by a formal halo."

And then says my friend, "Is not this the sort of a picture our age is painting?" When we have crowded in all the magnificence and splendor and beauty possible, if we admit the Christ at all it is not the real Christ, not the Christ of the Gospels, so severe in His demands of sacrifice, so regal in His moral authority, so insistent in His teachings of service, but a purely formal guest, distinguished from other men by the halo of a creed whose rule over the soul has been lost while we are "busy here and there" with the things that delight and entertain.

V
CHRIST AND THE COMMERCIAL WORLD

"Wist ye not that I must be about My Father's business?" — LUKE 2:49.

THE WORD "BUSINESS" is not in the original. I prefer the rendering, "Wist ye not that I must be about the things of my Father."

There are certain underlying concepts of Christianity which give to it any real worth and any abiding value it may have. Of these there are three which, in view of the message this morning, especially present themselves for consideration.

THE DEMAND FOR APPLIED CHRISTIANITY

1. One of these is this: Christianity to prove its worth, must assert itself in the practical affairs of a man's life in this world as well as in any ambition he may have for the life he hopes to have in the world to come.

In other words it must concern itself with the "needy now and now" as well as with the "sweet bye and bye." If it does not do this it is bound in the minds of men to lose its appeal very largely, if not altogether, so far as anything it may purport to do for them when the struggles and heart-aches of this world are over. If there is nothing practical in Christianity for this life it certainly forfeits its authority to speak for the life to come. It is a regrettable fact that no charge is urged more bitterly against the Church by the laboring man than this. They say they are asked to be submissive under their wrongs in this world with the hope that they will have their reward in the hereafter.

Now, just in so far as this charge is true, *if it is true at all,* the Church becomes guilty of utterly perverting the plain teachings of Jesus Christ. He was the author and the first exponent of Applied Christianity. It was Jesus who said, "Thou shalt love thy neighbor as thyself." This does not mean to pray for him in the pew on Sunday and then prey on him all the rest of the week. It does not mean to pile up a fortune by hard-pressure methods and then dole out a few paltry millions of conscience money to endow some philanthropical institution. It does not mean to hire somebody else to love them, but to go yourself and get acquainted with your neighbor and interest yourself in the callous-palmed toiler, the hard-working mechanic, the shiftless pauper, if you please, and the slave of every social curse, and love him into the place where God intended him to be.

In other words Christianity to be real must throw itself into the whole actual palpitating, throbbing life of society, bringing out into clear light the fine truth that real life consists not in the things we have, but in the life we give, and when society sees and puts its faith in this truth the law of the Cross will become the law of the commercial world, and the law of nations as well, and men shall take on the moral beauty of God and there will be peace and contentment and joy throughout the world.

"He's true to God who's true to man,
  Wherever wrong is done;
To the meanest and the weakest,

> *'Neath the all-beholding sun;*
> *That wrong is also done to us,*
> *And they are slaves most base,*
> *Whose love of right is for themselves,*
> *And not for all the race.*"

What Really Counts

2. *The second thing is this: The real test of Christianity is in life and not in profession.* It does not consist in going to church. When you're looking for the thermometer of a man's religion you need to watch his conduct six days in the week rather than his devotions on the seventh.

There are men in our day even as in Christ's who are up to the same old trick of making long prayers for pretense and spending the rest of their lives in the ghoulish work of devouring widows' houses. People say of them, as they said of Jacques Ferrand in Eugene Sue's "Mysteries of Paris," "Do you not observe how devout he is?"

It is not as a member of the Church but as a member of society that a man's religion is to be measured. Christianity in the ultimate does not consist in orthodoxy. It is a man's deeds and not his creeds by which other men measure his piety.

I would not underestimate the value of a creed. It is as necessary to a man's moral and spiritual being as a vertebra is to his body. But if the creed you profess doesn't produce a life that tallies with it, it is only so much sounding brass and tinkling cymbal. John Wesley said in his blunt way, "A man may be as orthodox as the Devil and just as wicked." We need orthopraxy as well as orthodoxy.

Business a Sacred Thing

3. *The third thing is this: We must disabuse our minds of this mischievous dualism which makes such drastic distinction between the so-called secular and sacred.* We need to rediscover the fact that in all things in which a Christian

man has a right to engage, he is doing the business of his Father in heaven, and that when the youthful Christ learned a trade and became a carpenter in Nazareth He was busied in the things of His Father just as much as when He questioned the doctors in His Father's temple. We need to understand that every profession and every trade and every work and every transaction that is not essentially dishonorable is, and ought to be made, a part of the business of God.

Hiram Goff called himself "A Shoemaker by the Grace of God," and said to the young parson, "I consider the making of a pair of shoes just as sacred and just as holy as the making of your sermon or the prayer you make in the house of God." And we need to realize that Hiram Goff was right, if only a man will conduct his business with a mind and a spirit like that of this quaint old "shoemaker by the grace of God."

In Old Testament times when they wanted a man to work on the curtains of the temple and the garments of the High Priest they chose Aholiab, and when they wanted a man to do the engraving and to carve in the silver and the gold they chose Bezaleel, and of these men it is said, "they were filled with the Spirit of God." And if our tailors and our jewelers and our tradesmen were men of that type the business of our day would become, as it ought to become, a means of communion with God and a ministry of the Gospel to reconcile the world unto Himself.

WE CONCLUDE THEREFORE, THAT BUSINESS, RIGHTLY CONCEIVED, IS ONE OF THE THINGS OF GOD AND ITS BASIC PRINCIPLES SHOULD BE ALTOGETHER CHRISTIAN.

Now, the question that stands out before us is this: Is business so conducted today?

Some say "Yes," and some say "No." Both in a sense are right, as the question is a relative one and neither answer can be given without certain qualifications. If compelled, however, to answer in a single word that word would be "No."

I am not going to be guilty of wholesale, sweeping condemnation, nor am I going to forget the immense debt which the world owes to its business men. There is hardly an institution of learning in the land nor an asylum for the afflicted that does not owe its existence and sustenance to the liberal endowment of wealth by men of business.

The man who with the fruits of honest industry builds a library, an art gallery, a university, an asylum, like Jacob digs a well for the refreshing of the ages—the Library stored with knowledge for generations yet unborn; the Art Gallery, with its inspiration for beauty and strength; the University, forever endowing the land with men of mental fitness; the Asylum, alleviating the woes of the unfortunate; all these, as long as time shall be, pay interest a thousandfold to humanity in coin imperishable because of the gift of philanthropic men.

What is Wrong

And yet there certainly must be something wrong; something unchristian somewhere when a common animal is better cared for than a common man; when a man wants to work and can find no work to do; when one man can't count his wealth, while his brother, as Bobby Burns says, "begs of him leave to toil," and who toils on till death, bringing to his family day by day less than a tenth of what is every day wasted in the rich man's house.

What is it about the commercial world that makes it so productive of dealings not on the level?

At a meeting of railroad presidents a few years ago where the famous "Gentlemen's Agreement" was propounded, President Marvin Hughitt of the Chicago and Northwestern road told his confreres a few things which, it seems to us, would be hard to forget. He said:

"Gentlemen, in your capacity as citizens, as individuals, I would never think of questioning your integrity; your word would be as good as your bond; I would trust you implicitly anywhere; but as railroad men I would not trust you across the street; I would not believe you under oath."

Sounds a bit severe doesn't it? But it's an indication of that *something* in the business world which seemingly presents a temptation too great for the tradesman to overcome, and as a result of it we find this particular sphere of life cursed with a large number of dishonorable practices of which men, when true to their better natures, would never be guilty; misrepresentation and deception; adulterations and imitations; false weights and short measures. These and other dishonesties have, in varying degree, cursed the realm of exchange ever since the time when prehistoric man first conceived the plan of barter.

"With what Measure you Mete"

Here's a good illustration; A baker living in a certain town bought his butter from a neighboring farmer. He became a little suspicious and so for several days he weighed the butter himself and found that the rolls of butter which the farmer brought were gradually diminishing in weight. This angered him and he had the farmer arrested.

The judge said to the farmer, "I presume you have weights."

"No, sir," replied the farmer.

"How, then, do you manage to weigh the butter that you sell?"

"Your honor," said the farmer, "that's easily explained. When the baker commenced buying his butter of me I thought I'd buy my bread of him, and I've been using his one-pound loaf as a weight for the butter I sell."

Of course back of all this is the innate depravity of the human heart. A thorough Christian will scorn the tricks of his trade. A really honest man would die rather than be dishonest. But the *something* to which we referred a moment ago which is largely responsible for the warped morality of the business world is, I am inclined to think, the tiger principle of competition. It is this ravenous tooth and bloody claw method of buying and selling that makes it hard for a man to be a Christian business man.

Here is a merchant who says he never goes to bed at night without being afraid that some competitor will steal his business before morning.

COMPETITION OR CO-OPERATION

Competition ought to give way to the more sensible and only divine system of co-operation. Without co-operation of some sort men will, under the stress of competition, be eternally tearing at each other's throats. As long as the commercial world is engaged in a desperate competitive struggle to see who shall be on top some men are bound to go to the bottom, and the average man is not going there if by any method which obtains in the commercial world generally he can keep himself from it.

"But," you say, "competition is the law of nature." It is the law of nature. It is the law of trees, but men are not trees. It is the law of weeds in the corn patch, but men are not weeds. It is the law of beasts, but men are not brutes. It is the law of nature, but it is not the law of Jesus, and the whole commercial enterprise as now conducted, much in consequence of it, presents a program of trickery and deception, and sometimes heartless oppression in which the whole of society is involved."

The trouble with us all is that we are looking no further than is necessary to see a bargain, and no matter how much we love each other in the prayermeeting room we are always sure to keep our eye on each other in the business room:

WHAT BUSINESS NEEDS

What the commercial world needs is Christ. To admit that you cannot do business on Christian principles is to admit that you are engaged in a dishonest enterprise. The question, "What would Jesus do?" is practical. It is practical for the pulpit, practical for the home, and it is practical for the store and the factory, and every business man, if he is a thorough Christian, will ask it. There is a beautiful legend in the Greek Church that when Jesus ascended and the cloud received Him out of sight He floated away and came back to earth again clothed in a different form, and that He still walks about visiting the haunts of man. It is a beautiful legend and it enshrines a glorious truth.

Jesus is still here. Oh, that men might see Him and give Him His rightful place in the affairs of life. Then, indeed, would dishonesty, and graft and greed and sin of every kind, with the sorrow and suffering it entails flee away before the advancing power of His love and His justice, which will yet one day cause His will to be done on earth as it is in heaven.

"When God made this world He took precious care," some one has said, "to see to it that it would pay to do right."

Oh, that men might see it—that Godliness is profitable. If I were forced to believe that my Christ was a hindrance to the onswinging betterment of this world in any sphere my head would hang forever down; but because I have seen Him everywhere—seen Him in Society; seen Him in the Home; seen Him in the hard, clashing life of the market place, and know that men can live Him even there, I will lift up my head for I know that sure as God is in the world the glad day of our redemption draweth nigh.

Have you seen Him? And have you allowed Him to take His rightful place in your life? If you have not done this then let Him take that place this morning—in your business, in your social relations, in your home, and everywhere else, and remember that the time will come when He will mean more to you than all the world besides.

Vanderbilt had what men call a successful career, but when he was dying with his millions he called to his bedside his faithful old gardener, who had been an earnest Christian all his life, and said to him:

"Will you sing for me?"

"What shall I sing?" said the old man.

"Sing for me," said the dying millionaire:

"Come ye sinners, poor and needy,
Weak and wounded, sick and sore."

And the old gardener sang it for him, and then the great merchant prince repeated the words.

And he was gone into the eternal world.

VI

THE LOST WORD

OR

THE NAME OF JESUS

"There is none other name given under heaven whereby we must be saved." —ACTS 4:12.

HERMAS, AS THE STORY GOES, was the son of rich, old Demetrius. He was spending his youth in riotous living in Antioch until he came in contact with John of Antioch by whom he was converted to Christianity. He at once renounced his life of luxury and dissipation and wild revel and because of his belief gave up his father's house where he was given to understand he was not welcome if he forsook the gods for Christ.

For a time he was happy and he thought to give his life in service for the church. But after a while the world commenced to beckon him again; he found himself getting a bit weary of prayers and fasting and services. He had grown careless and a good deal of his earlier joy and peace had slipped away from him and he began to wonder if he had not been disillusioned and robbed.

In this mood, he came away from the service one day dissatisfied and at the corner of the street a beautiful, yellow-haired girl, one of his old companions, put out her hand and caught him by the sleeve and smiled in his face.

"Stay," she said, "and laugh a bit with us. I know who you are; you are the son of Demetrius. You must have bags of gold. Why do you look so black? Love is alive yet."

Hermas shook off her hand, but not ungently.

"I don't know what you mean," he said. "You are mistaken in me. I am poorer than you are."

But as he passed on, he felt the warm touch of her fingers through the cloth on his arm, and it seems as if it stirred again the old life that once was within. But he passed on and turning to the left he wandered into the grove of Daphne and sat down by one of its springs. And as he sat there a pagan priest came along and sat down by his side and told him of how the Emperor Hadrian once had his fortune told by dipping a leaf into this spring. And the old priest plucked a twig from a laurel tree and dipped it in. The leaf on it turned yellow, a bud on the stem commenced to swell and on the surface of the leaf there was a tracing of a wreath. These omens Hermas read to mean wealth, pleasure and fame.

"I promise that you shall have all these" said the pagan priest, "but you must give to me in return one thing, just one thing, a single word, the name of Him whom you profess to worship. Let me take it from your mind so that you will forget it, and from your lips so that you will never be able to speak it. Do you consent?"

"Yes, I consent," said Hermas. And then he fell into a deep sleep. And when he awoke he knew his life had changed; how, he knew not, but he was buoyant and free once more.

He started straight home and the servants ran to meet him and told him his old father lay dying and was calling for him. And the old man said, "My son, I am dying and my soul is empty, but you have something which I feel must satisfy me. You were willing to give up your life for your faith. Tell it to me—your secret—before I go." And Hermas said, "Father, it is very simple. You must believe in—you must believe in—you must believe in—," but the name of Jesus, the name of Christ refused to come to his lips. And the light behind his father's eyes went out.

Upon his father's death all his vast riches fell, of course, to Hermas. He married a beautiful girl, Athenais, and a lovely child came to them. Everything was his, wealth, honor, beauty, and love. But there was something that oppressed him like an invisible burden. They talked it over and thought that possibly they had not been grateful enough and they said "we will express thanks for all the good fortune that has come to us," and they knelt to pray and Hermas began. He dwelt for a moment upon the blessings that were theirs and closed his prayer, saying, "For all good gifts, for all perfect gifts, for love, for life, for the world, we praise, we bless, we thank—." There was no one to thank: the word was lost.

One day after a winning run at the chariot races, he lifted his beautiful boy into his chariot to share the honors with him but the horses became frightened and the little lad was hurled to the ground and when Hermas looked he was lying like a broken flower on the sand. They carried him home. Two days he lingered and as he was dying they fell on their knees and Hermas prayed: "Out of the depths we cry for pity; the light of our eyes is fading—the child is dying. Oh, spare the child's life, thou merciful—" and then a deathly blank. They could neither think of nor utter the name of Christ.

"Long ago," said Hermas, "I knew something. I think it would have helped me. But I have forgotten it."

While he was speaking a slave entered the room and told him that John of Antioch was waiting out in the peristyle and the old heathen priest Marcion was trying to turn him away.

"Come," said Hermas to his wife, "let us go to him."

Out in the hall the two men were standing, Marcion with sneering lips, tormenting John of Antioch, who stood silent and patient. As Hermas approached, John of Antioch said, "My son, you did not send for me, but I have come hearing that you are in trouble."

"It is true," answered Hermas, "we are in trouble. Our child is dying. In all this house, in all the world, there is no one that can help us. I knew something long ago, when I was with you—a word, a name—in which we might have found hope. But I have lost it. I gave it to this man. He has taken it away from me forever."

He pointed to Marcion. The old man's lips curled scornfully. "A word, a name!" he sneered. "What was it? A thing of air; a word, a name that only a fool would prize!"

"Servant of demons, be still!" The voice of John rang clear, like a trumpet, through the hall. "There is a name which none shall dare to take in vain. There is a name which none can lose without being lost. There is a name at which the devils tremble. Go quickly, before I speak it!"

And then John of Antioch gave back to Hermas the name of Christ, the name of God, and they knelt down and prayed and even as they prayed they heard the little child calling for its mother.

WHAT HIS NAME WILL DO

If ever a warning was sounded for the Christian who yearns for the flesh pots of Egypt and those to whom the world is beckoning with its bewitching smile, it is the story of Henry VanDyke's "Lost Word." And if there was ever a call to those who have gotten away from their first love to come and find again the touch of His hand, and the sound of His voice, and feel again the throb of His heart, it is in this story that I have told you this morning.

There's never a guilty conscience that NAME will not relieve; there's never a temptation that NAME will not overcome; there's never a joy that NAME will not make the sweeter; there's never a sorrow that NAME will not heal; there's never a bereavement that NAME will not sanctify; there's never a fear at the thought of death that NAME will not chase away. And if you have never known that NAME or have known and then forgotten it and allowed the meaning of it to go out of your life, then you are poor indeed; much more so than God ever meant you to be.

1. NEVER A GUILTY CONSCIENCE THAT NAME WILL NOT RELIEVE;

> *"I dug a grave and laid within*
> *It's secret depths one secret sin;*
> *I closed the grave and know full well*
> *That day I shut myself in hell."*

For I do not know what hell is, either here or hereafter, if it is not Conscience in all of its divine, terrific power let loose on the human soul.

Herod can behead John but he can't silence the voice of Conscience. Lady MacBeth can cry "Out damned spot!" but not all of Neptune's ocean can wipe away the bloody stain nor all the perfumes of Arabia sweeten the little lily-white hand that did the bloody deed.

ALONE WITH CONSCIENCE

Do you know the poem, "I sat alone with my Conscience?" And isn't it true that when you do you have to say with the poet,

> *"My conscience hath a thousand several tongues,*
> *And every tongue brings in a several tale,*
> *And every tale condemns me for what I really am."*

But when the One, whose Name is Jesus, comes He says

"Peace, be still," to the troubled soul, for he comes from the Cross with the blood of reconciliation to "sprinkle the heart," as the word of God says, "from an evil conscience" and you will know then out of a blessed experience what it means to serve God, as Paul said he served Him, with a conscience pure and undefiled.

2. NEVER A TEMPTATION THAT NAME WILL NOT HELP YOU OVERCOME.
For
> "Satan trembles when he sees
> The weakest saint upon his knees."

Do you recall that magic flower given to Ulysses by the god whose name was Mercury and the wonderful power it had to resist the sorceries of the enchantress. Circe had turned all his companions into swine, who as Milton writes in his "Comus,"
> Not once perceive their foul disfigurement
> But boast themselves more comely than before;
> And all their friends and native home forget,
> To roll with pleasure in a sensual sty."

But when Ulysses came he had with him the magic flower which made powerless the charms of the enchantress, for when Circe gave him the wine and cried,
> "Hence! seek the sty and wallow with thy friends."

he drew his sword and made her beg for mercy.
What a rare and precious specimen that must have been! But for the child of God that flower is the Rose of Sharon; it is the Lily of the Valley, pure, sweet and strong; and no matter what the enchantment be; the wine when it sparkles, the eyes that look visions of lust; the world, the flesh, and the Devil, with all their bewitching pull; let it be what it will, the Name of Jesus with all it can mean in your life, is

strong to deliver and will save you out of the very mouth of hell.

3. Never a joy that Name will not make the sweeter.

I tried, one time to plead with a thoughtless, careless worldling and to show him the folly of his way; how he was missing the true joys of life. And he said, "Fun? I have had more d—n fun in the last hour than you ever had in your whole life." And scarcely more than a year had passed when he put a pistol to his temple and sent a bullet whizzing through his brain.

Fun? What do you mean by that word? Some one has wisely said, "The Devil has no happy old people." Some of you may think that you are having a jolly good time now, but the time will come when you will see your mistake, and the things you now think are full of fun will turn to Apples of Sodom and be full of ashes and bitterness.

God's Love Greater Than A Mother's

Some of us will have to know God better than we do. If your child should come and say, "Mother, I know you love me and you are wiser than I and I want to do just what you say; I want to submit my will to yours," what would you say and do? Would you say, "Now, I've got my child just where I want him, and I'll make it hard for him and fill his life with everything that is unlovely." No, but you would say, "God bless you, my child, for that trust," and you would proceed at once to fill its life with all that is sweet and happy and wholesome and joyous and strong.
But listen:

"What is more tender than a mother's love
To her sweet child fondling in her arms,
What arguments need her compassions move,
To hear its cries and help it in its harms?
Yet if the tenderest mother were possessed
Of all the love within her single breast,

> *Of all the mothers since the world began,*
> *'Tis nothing to the love of God to man."*
> (JOHN BYROM, 1680 A.D.)

Well, my friend, God is better than the best mother that ever lived, and if you want your life made rich with joy like that, just make that life over to Him whose Name is Jesus and see what He will do.

4. NEVER A SORROW THAT NAME WILL NOT HEAL.

God knows there is sorrow enough in the world. Man seems born to it as the sparks fly upward. Trouble and disappointment; burdens and sorrow everywhere.

Look at the Home; the homes of every class, especially of the rich and the affluent. Homes like the one where the mother of Harry Thaw had to live; homes like that of Yerkes of Chicago, or of Post, the Cereal King. But why multiply names?

I have been driven through the fashionable residence portion of some of our larger cities and my companion has pointed out residence after residence and said, "A divorce there. A suicide there. A drunken, gambling son there," until it seemed like I was riding through a graveyard of virtue and honor and every home was a mausoleum of misery.

And yet in one of those homes I found a character so brave, so patient, so gracious, so noble and so chaste I could not help but marvel, and when I said, "Tell me the secret of it all," it was the same sweet story of Jesus and the meaning of His Name.

Why bear the burdens and sorrows of life alone? It is like the old lady who insisted on holding her heavy bundle while riding on a passenger train.

5. NEVER A BEREAVEMENT THAT NAME WILL NOT SANCTIFY.

I wish you might know the story of Todd Hall, a one-time detective in the city of Baltimore. He was a very sinful man. He went one day into one of Mr. Moody's meetings to arrest a criminal but something Mr. Moody said arrested Todd Hall and he became a Christian. His wife said she would go with him into the Church and his little daughter said she would go too. A little later Todd Hall became a preacher as well as a detective.

One day when my friend Dr. M.B. Wharton returned to Baltimore a neighbor said to him, "Todd Hall's little girl is dead." And Dr. Wharton said, "Has it hurt Todd any? Has it affected his power?" and the man said, "Oh no, but you ought to see him and you ought to hear him now."

When the doctor said, "Mr. Hall, your little girl is dying," he just knelt down and said, "Dear and ever blessed God, You gave her to me and You loved her and saved her, and now I give her back to Thee." And as the doctor said, "Mr. Hall, she is breathing her last now," he held her little hand in his and looking up began to sing with a sweet tenor voice, which was his, "Bear her away on your snowy wings to her eternal home," and she was gone.

And Todd Hall never knew what it was to preach before; he never knew what it was to work in the service of God. God just sanctified the bereavement to him and he arose from his knees transfigured by His marvelous grace and power.

Oh, my friends, why look upon the face of God through the clouded glass of your own bitter tears and think Him cruel, unkind and indifferent, when through the Name that is above every name He will make your deepest trial and your severest affliction to be unto you the means of grace exceeding great arid precious.

6. Never a fear at the thought of death that Name will not chase away.

Say what you will, my friend, but it is not an easy thing to face death when you have no faith and are without God and without hope in the world, but no man, when dying, has ever felt sorry he opened his life to the meaning of the Name of Jesus.

Some day for you and me the journey will end and it will not end merely with a hole in the ground, as Clemenceau, the Tiger of France, said it was to end for him. The best that Robert G. Ingersol could think was of "faith trying to see a star," and "hope trying to catch the sound of an angel's wing." But it was a cold and cheerless conclusion to which he came, for he said, standing as he was beside the coffin of his brother, "whether amid ocean or amid the breakers of the farther shore a wreck must mark at last the end of each and every life."

Sailing Without a Pilot

A westbound Atlantic Steamer was having a serious time in the dense fog off the coast of Newfoundland. The officers had completely lost their bearings; they knew well they were in treacherous waters, and for three days crew and passengers were filled with anxiety and suspense. On the fourth day the ship, from main deck to steerage, rang with cheers. Out of the thick gloom a little sloop had come bearing a pilot and, as the great grizzled monarch of the seas clambered up the distressed vessel's side and took the wheel, both passengers and crew knew deliverance had come. Can you imagine them refusing to take the pilot on!

Shortly after Wilhelm II was crowned Emperor of Germany there appeared that famous picture, "Dropping the Pilot." One of the first things Kaiser Wilhelm did after ascending the throne was to break with Bismarck, the Iron Chancellor, whose sterling statesmanship had made Germany what she was. The waters were rough and the storm clouds were hanging low and the great ship was standing out to sea. Alongside was the pilot's boat, so familiar to all who cross the ocean; the pilot, Bismarck, was going down the ladder. From that hour, surely and sometimes swiftly, Germany was riding to destruction.

What is true of the ship of state is equally true of the bark of one's own life. To sail life's sea without the Great Pilot on board is a sad and serious mistake, for all too often the waters will be storm-tossed, and treacherous. Whatever else you do, don't start out without the Pilot and don't drop Him when out to sea. Remember that you will need Him most when crossing the bar and amid the breakers of the farther shore.

"Jesus, Savior, pilot me
Over life's tempestuous sea;

And

When at last I near the shore
And the fearful breakers roar
Twixt me and the peaceful rest,
Then while leaning on thy breast
May I hear thee say to me
'Fear not, I will pilot thee.'''

"Sunset and the evening star,
And one clear call for me,
And may there be no moaning of the bar
When I put out to sea.

"Twilight and evening bell,
And after that the dark
And may there be no sadness of farewell
When I embark.

"For though from out the bourne of time and place
The flood may bear me far,
I hope to see my Pilot face to face
When I have crossed the bar."

VII
BENAIAH IN THE LION'S PIT

"And Benaiah went down and slew a lion in a pit on a snowy day." —II SAMUEL 23:20.

BRAVERY IS ONE of the essentials of high character. The world always takes off its hat to a brave man—the man who always delivers, without witness or before the world, and doesn't take his bravery out simply in advertising it.

In the days of the American Revolution some men were sitting on a log and one fellow was telling what he would do if the Red Coats came—how he would show them a thing or two. Just then came the "rub-a-dub-dub; rub-a-dub-dub" of the Red Coats down along the roadway. They all ran, but this fellow was the speediest of the lot. In jumping over a fence he lit on a rake and the handle flew up and hit him in the back of the head, and he cried, "Hurrah for King George. I surrender!"

Goliath was a mouthing braggart. David was a man of five smooth pebbles and a sling. And so Benaiah was a man of deeds and not of words. He went down into a pit and slew a lion on a snowy day. No fuss, no feathers about it.

He simply did it. Duty called and Benaiah was there with the goods. He leaped down to face the roaring brute knowing that out of that pit only one would come up alive. God must have had a pardonable pride in writing in the record the brief statement of the exploit of this brave man. God never writes a nobody in His Word. The world forgets all too soon. There ought to be no such thing as an unsung hero. But there have been others and many of them whose daring deeds the world has never ceased to sing. We think of Horatius defending the bridge at Thermopylae[1] against a whole army; of Richard Couer de Leon [sic] braving the Saracen host without finding a single enemy to stand against his assault; of Robert Bruce crushing with one blow the helmet and the head of Sir Henry Bohun in sight of the whole army of England; of Arnold von Winklereid, throwing himself upon the Austrian spears and breaking the ranks for the patriots of Switzerland to rush on through to victory; of Sergeant Alvin York, if you please, in the World War, capturing single handed 132 Germans, of whom three were officers, taking 35 machine guns, and killing, because he was compelled to do so, no less than 25 of the enemy.

It was out of material like that that Benaiah was made. He was known as one of David's "mighty men." He was a valiant man with many illustrious deeds doubtless to his credit. But our text tells us of one that would be as gratefully remembered by the members of the community as the killing of a man-eating tiger by the natives in India.

THE FIGHT IN THE PIT

It was a snowy day. Not a day of Florida sunshine with the air vocal with the whistling of birds and redolent with

---

1. The Roman Horatius defended the bridge over the Tiber River against the Etruscans, 509 BC; Thermopylae was the pass 300 Spartans held against invading Persians in 480 BC. —*Ed. 2016.*

the perfume of orange blossoms, of oleanders and ever-blooming roses. Not one of those days in the Springtime of the North when your veins are filled with pulsing blood and your muscles tingle with elasticity and you feel like you could whip the world. But it was a cold day, a day like that

> *"When Dick the plowman, blows his nail,*
> *And milk comes frozen home in pail."*

And it was on such a day that Benaiah went down into a pit and slew a lion. It was a lion doubtless that had been preying upon the livestock and even the inhabitants as they went in and out of the town. Whether he made this pit his lair or had stumbled into it matters not.

One day, and it was a snowy day, there came a roar that made the very air tremble as well as the neighbors who were toasting their toes and burning their knees over the fire. Benaiah jumps to his feet. His opportunity had come. He had said, "If I ever get a chance, I'll make that old lion feel sorry he was ever born." And out into the hurtling snow and the biting air he goes; alone, with no one to cheer him on, he comes nearer and nearer to the pit with the lion in it. He leans over the edge, and aware of his presence, he is greeted with a ferocious growl by the brute who had been the terror of the countryside for many a day.

There is not a second of hesitation. With a prayer to Israel's God, Benaiah leaps down into the pit. There's a roar, a lashing of tail, a gleaming of teeth, and a spring. And, now, look! The lion's claws are buried in Benaiah's shoulders; but with one hand on his upper jaw and the other on his lower, Benaiah literally tears his face apart. There is one deep-seated groan and the lion is down with his head bathed in his own blood. And Benaiah, who went down in a pit and slew a lion on a snowy day, comes up and back a victor.

Need I tell you this morning in the house of God that we

all have battles like that to fight? Need I remind you that that man down in the pit in his fight to death with a lion is a type, a figure in his experience of what every man must go through? There's a lion in some pit for every one of us.

Character is made much like the growth of the sturdy oak. The storms and the buffeting of the winds seem to be essential elements in the process of its development. We can hardly expect to escape all the struggle and the warfare of life, nor are we sure it is a thing to be desired. At any rate there are victories to be won by moral courage and spiritual weapons that are much greater and nobler than any of the exploits of heroes like those mentioned a moment ago.

Yes, there's a lion in some pit for every one of us.

I. THERE IS THE PIT OF HEREDITY. You will find an interesting study of this pre-natal influence if you will compare the history of the Edwards family with that of the Jukes family. The one gave to us nearly 1,400 college professors, lawyers, authors, ministers, and social servants in general, while the other gave us 1,200 imbeciles, criminals and other social scourges.

This means that this thing we call Heredity is a boost for some and an almost insurmountable handicap for others. The mother of Nero was a murderess. Byron, the poet, could be pitied and even loved a bit more if people knew his family.

But where these, and many like them, have failed, others there are
>"Who break their birth's invidious bar
>   And grasp the skirts of happy chance,
>And breast the blows of circumstance,
>   And grapple with their evil star."

To Him that Overcometh

I think of Demosthenes battling with his impediment of speech until the whole Athenian world was thrilled with his unrivaled oratory.

I think of Steinmetz, the wizard of Schenectady, with the cruel deformity given him by nature, and how he rose above it until he stands today a dominant figure in the realm of science.

I think of Robert Louis Stevenson in the field of literature, who, as a child with his little weak chest inherited from his mother, coughed many a night the weary darkness through; who "never had a fair chance" and had to say, "All my life I have wakened sick and gone to bed weary," writing in bed, in hemorrhages, and when his head swam for weakness, but who with the courage of the unconquerable God did his work unflinchingly and left for us a legacy of gems richer and more imperishable than which the Muse of Literature ever inspired.

What a motto must have been his!

> *"Out of the night that covers me,*
>   *Black as the Pit from pole to pole,*
> *I thank whatever Gods there be*
>   *For an unconquerable soul.*
> *In the fell clutch of circumstance*
>   *I have not winced nor cried aloud;*
> *Under the bludgeoning of chance*
>   *My head: is bloody but unbowed.*
> *It matters not how straight the gate,*
>   *How charged with punishment the scroll;*
> *I am the master of my fate;*
>   *I am the captain of my soul!"*
>   [William Ernest Henley, "Invictus," 1888]

In the realm of character we must think in legions in any attempt to count the overcomers. Gloucester had no right to argue that because he was born mean he would yield to his impulses.

II. There is the Pit of Environment. Ah, it seems that circumstance is a stranger to impartiality.

What can one expect of Oliver Twist living in Fagin's den or of a lad born in and environed by the slums and the underworld life of some great city?

And yet I think now of one such born and reared in the outskirts of New York City, knowing nothing but biting poverty; hearing nothing but profanity; taught to steal as a fine art; no education; no helpful influence of any kind; everything pulling him down until he became a poor, staggering, drunken river-thief, and yet who, in battle royal through the grace of God, became a man of whom the pastor of the great Fifth Avenue Presbyterian Church of New York City said that he had more power for God over the people of that metropolitan city than all the pastors combined, and whose death brought endless streams of people, rich and poor, who piled flowers on his coffin so high they hid the pulpit, and beneath that pyramid of flowers slept Jerry McAuley.

There are other Pits, many of them.

III. There is the Pit of Discouragement. When a man allows himself to be discouraged he is already nine-tenths beaten.

IV. There is the Pit of Pride. Wasn't it Coleridge who said,
> "And the Devil did grin; for his darling sin
> Is pride that apes humility."

V. There is the Pit of Envy.
That
> "Envy which turns pale
> And sickens even if a friend prevail."

VI. But I am thinking more especially now of another pit. IT IS THE PIT OF APPETITE, WHERE THE LION OF PASSION IS TO BE MET; the pit where John B. Gough, and John G. Wooley, and Samuel Hopkins Hadley met the beast of strong drink, and where Philip Quinn, and Howard Cadle, and James Killgore came to death-grips with the curse of gambling. And when I read the story of their struggles and how they stood at last with their foot on the neck of the lion, I know then that there is victory for every one who must go down into that pit if only they do battle as these men did.

I am not going to make any mistake this morning when I say there is an evil something down deep, shall I say, within every one of us—a power of lion-like strength. For some it may be one thing; for others another thing.

Bobbie Burns, the idol poet of Scotland, who could write poems like "The Cotter's Saturday Night," and "A Man's a Man for a' that," one time said of himself that he could no more resist the whiskey jug even though he knew an actual adder was coiled in its neck than he could overthrow Gibraltar with an iron crowbar.

But whatever that thing may be, not one of us, whether we be old or young, will ever be what I trust in our better moments we want to be; we will never be safe until we have done what Benaiah did and gone down into the pit that is within us and torn to pieces the thing that threatens the very life of our soul.

THE INEVITABLE ALTERNATE

And we have this fact to face; that if that thing is not slain we will be slain by it.

I entered one time into an exhibition where, among other unusual and awesome feats, a wild animal tamer was giving a demonstration of his power over a full-grown lion that had been captured for him on the plains of Africa. It was said to be the most ferocious beast in captivity, and was advertised as "The Untamable." Four men stood, one at each corner of the cage, with irons heated red hot at one end to be used against the beast in case of emergency.

The trainer entered the cage armed only with a chair, a whip, and a small pistol from which he fired a few blank cartridges. The brute resented the intrusion and sprang at the man with a terrifying growl, but the man soon showed himself master of the situation. Their eyes met and the beast was cowed. The man drove him into a corner, made him jump over the chair and through a hoop handed in to him, and the people were awed by the daring sight and gave the man great applause.

It was only a few weeks after that time when I read in my newspaper of the fatal attempt of a similar exhibition. The lion had been driven into his corner as usual, and then without a second of warning made a savage lunge, accompanied by a ferocious, blood-curdling growl, and before the guardsmen could act buried his claws in the trainer's shoulders and tore his throat out with his angry jaws.

Men and women, let us beware how we play, how we trifle with passion, with appetite, with sin of any kind. There is a battle you must fight; there's a lion you must slay if you don't want to be slain by it. Go down into the pit. Don't be cowardly. Ah, yes, you'll hear the growlings of the brute and feel almost the lashings of his tail, but go down, drive the beast into the corner, and slay, utterly slay it, as you value the life of your soul.

A God-Built Man

"But," you say, "it's so hard." Yes, it was hard for Benaiah too. It was a snowy day, and the beast was maddened with hunger, for food had been hard to find. It was a snowy day, and the bottom of the pit was slippery, and Benaiah must have kept his foothold with great difficulty as the lion sprang with threatening jaws upon him.

But there's something in the narrative we haven't mentioned yet. Benaiah's name means something. Names always did in those days. It's not so with us. We want beautiful names. We call our children "Gwendolyn," "Clarissa," "Geraldine," and other sweet-sounding titles which have no meaning, but in those days they gave a man a name in keeping with the traits that were strongest in his character. I wonder what your name would sound like if you were given a name in that way. "Judah" means "praise," "Jacob" means "cunning," and "Benaiah" means something. It means literally "The Man Whom God Built."

Benaiah was born of God, and being thus born he was God-made, and God-strengthened, and God-undergirded, and God-nerved, and it was in the Name of the Lord God of Israel that he "went down into a pit and slew a lion on a snowy day," and when you go that way there can be no doubt about the issue of the conflict. To go down any other way is to go down to defeat—down to death.

Possible—to go down in the Name and the strength of Benaiah's God? Well, what is this we read, that "the eyes of the Lord are running to and fro throughout the whole world to show Himself strong in behalf of them whose heart is right toward Him."

Up from the Pit

Thank God, the man who went down in a pit and slew a lion on a snowy day is a type of another Benaiah, One who on the grayest, dreariest, dullest, darkest day the world has ever known went down into the pit that was dug by your sin and mine and there engaged in mortal combat with the great adversary of the soul, "who," we are told, "goeth about as a roaring lion, seeking whom he may devour." He went alone, for "of the people there was none with Him." So alone He was that He felt Himself forsaken of God; and there, single-handed, with no one even to cheer Him on, while all the cohorts of hell were arrayed against Him, He met and slew the lion, the great dragon, the prince of darkness. He utterly overcame him, and

"Up from the pit He arose
With a mighty triumph o'er His foes;
He arose a Victor from the dark domain,
And He lives, forever with His saints to reign;
Hallelujah, Christ arose!"

Don't go down alone. Take the Almighty Christ, the glorious Son of God with you and come up with Him in victory. Make Him your constant companion; catch step and keep march with Him through life, and He will set the joy-bells ringing in your soul, and life will no longer be merely "an empty dream," "a dreary round of existence," "a waste of wearisome hours," measured by "figures on a dial," but redeemed and glorified in Christ by holier definitions, it will be a thing to which you can say when the last grain is running through its hour glass here and the shadows begin to deepen round about you,

"Say not 'Good Night,' but in
Some brighter clime,
Bid me 'Good Morning'."

VIII
THE POWER OF HABIT

"For the good that I would I do not; but the evil which I would not, that I do." —ROMANS 7:19.

SOME YEARS AGO Henry Clay Trumbull went into a theater over in London to see a noted wild animal trainer give an exhibition of his power over the beasts he had gotten from the jungles. He had lions and leopards and hyenas and tigers and he put them all through their part of the performance with remarkable skill. And now the closing act of the exhibition has come and I recite it so far as I am able in Mr. Trumbull's own words.

The bills had announced the appearance of a huge boa-constrictor thirty-five feet long. A wire screen is placed before the audience and while the weird strains of an oriental band of music come stealing through the trees the curtain rises upon an Indian woodland scene. In the foreground is nature's velvety carpet that shines like an emerald from Muzo. Yonder at one side is the treacherous thicket, and shooting up from it are the tall trees, from which stagger the thickly woven vines with their large clusters of tropical fruit that shine in the summer's sun like huge drops of ruby, and pearl, and topaz, and opal.

A rustling noise is heard, a stirring of the foliage, and a huge serpent is seen winding its way from the undergrowth. Fifteen feet of its ponderous body is now out on the stage, when suddenly it stops; its head erect, its forked tongue shot out, its eyes flashing fire. The audience shrinks back and the lips of some utter a cry, but the serpent seems unaware of their presence. Is he aware of anything? Yes, from the other side of the stage emerges a man. They advance toward each other, the serpent with measured windings and the man with cat-like stealth; until the big snake stops, lifts up its head and shoots out its forked tongue. Then eyes meet eyes—and the man is master of the beast. The serpent quails and at the bidding of the man goes through a series of frightful contortions. It obeys every command of the man who seems to have it absolutely in his power. At a sign it moves upon him and begins to coil itself about his feet. Higher and higher it rises, coil upon coil, until man and serpent seem to be one, with the serpent's hissing head reared above them both. The audience burst out into thunderous applause. The man gave a cry from within the coils and the crowd thought it was but another command and again it cheered. But their cheers were frozen upon their lips, the trainer's cry was the wail of his death agony. Those cold, slimy coils had embraced him for the last time, and as they began to tighten the horror-struck audience heard bone after bone crack until the hideous monster of the jungle had crushed the life out of the man in its embrace.

That man had gotten that reptile when it was but three or four days old. He had handled it daily and carried it in his arms when it was young. For twenty-five years he had fed it and trained it until it seemed harmless altogether, but it lived to crush out his life at last.

What an illustration of the text we have chosen this

morning: "For the good that I would, that I do not; but the evil which I would not, that I do."

THE HIGHER VERSUS THE LOWER MAN

Theologians have argued a great deal as to whether the "I" who is here speaking refers to the regenerated or the unregenerated individual. This is a matter they must settle among themselves; but one thing I know, the conflict between man's double nature does not cease with regeneration.

"Every man is a double and the lower man grips at the very throat of the higher and spiritual man." And sometimes the struggle is pathetic indeed.

Said a man to me the other day, "When I married my wife she was a beautiful girl. Our home was a paradise. Two beautiful girls were born to us, and then I began to drink. I broke my wife's heart. I brought the consuming disease which fed upon her vitals. One day she said, "I am dying and I want you to promise me two things before I pass away." I said, "Yes, anything." "First," she said, "promise me you will be kind to the children." I promised it. "Now, promise me that you will meet me in heaven." I put my hand upon her forehead and I swore by Him that sat upon the throne above that I would never touch intoxicating drink again. And then he said, "within six weeks I was a drunkard once more."

Oh, the countless thousands of men drawn by the irresistible power of passion down into the way that leads to swift and soul-damning destruction. Men like Lord Byron, with "a fire in their bosom that burns like some volcanic blaze," trying to do, but powerless; striving not to do, only to do the thing they know will prove to be their undoing; resolution broken; determination baffled; will-power gone; manhood dishonored; hoping it is all a dream, and crying like the man in Solomon's Proverb, "When shall I awake!" only to say in the morning, "I will seek it yet again," until like the man of the text he cries, "Oh wretched man that I am, who shall deliver me from the body of this death." It was the picture of a struggle something like this that was in the writer's mind when he wrote the words of the text, "For the good that I would, I do not; but the evil which I would not, that I do."

Austerlitz or Gettysburg

Life for the holiest man is warfare, and sometimes it's a long drawn-out Austerlitz or Gettysburg, with the fortunes of the hour in the balance. Sometimes it is victory, and sometimes, alas, it is defeat.

Two things especially make the fight a hard one.

1. Because of the downward pull of moral gravitation. An old lady in the backwoods was asked what she thought of the doctrine of Total Depravity, and she said she thought it was a very good doctrine if people would only live up to it. But just here is our trouble; we're living altogether too much up to it, or rather down to it, — this something that's very much akin, at least, to this thing the theologians call Total Depravity.

It's easier to go down hill than it is to go up. Say what you will, but the law of degeneration which you see running through all nature runs through human nature as well. There is a downward tendency, a downward thrust, a downward pull against which you have to fight in climbing up. That's why it's easier sometimes to do wrong than it is to do right.

2. The other thing that makes the fight hard is the power of habit. We all know something about this. Carlyle calls it the deepest law of human nature. If it is reasonable to expect the Colorado River to lift itself with the power of its own swift-flowing current out of the Royal Gorge, which by its incessant flow it has cut out of the rocky hills through

which it has run for ages, then it will be reasonable to expect the stream of life to lift itself by its own power out of the channel which by the incessant action of its thoughts and feelings and appetites has been made for it, and through which it too has run for years.

Habit works both ways. You may cultivate good habits as well as evil ones. It may, therefore, prove itself to be your benediction or your curse. It may build for you a palace or a dungeon.

But it is a red light I am swinging before you this morning. That evil habit of yours, if not resisted, will become a necessity in your life. We act more from habit than we do from reflection, as Paley said.

You were profane—you spoke with an oath yesterday, to your own disgust and that of your friends. You didn't exactly mean to, in fact you had determined not to, but the demon habit uttered his harsh command and the oath flew from your mouth like an arrow from the tight-strung bow of Ulysses. You told a lie yesterday. It was not premeditated. The one before it was to be the last. You lost again at the gaming table, or you may have won and the money is burning now in your purse. Well, it is true, as Johnson has well said, "The chains of habit are generally too small to be felt until they are too strong to be broken."

You recall the story of Dr. Jekyll and Mr. Hyde? The good doctor succeeded in concocting a powerful drug by which he could transform himself into an evil monster by the name of Mr. Hyde. And do you remember how the thing grew upon him? And how at last without the use of the drug at all he would turn into Mr. Hyde in spite of himself, and as it thus grew easier to become Mr. Hyde, it became correspondingly harder to get back again into Dr. Jekyll, his better self, until at last he died in the wicked character of Mr. Hyde.

And so it is, an evil habit grows. Even the Greeks knew

that listening to the song of the Sirens meant hopeless shipwreck upon the bone-strewn shore.

And so many a man has sailed the seas of secret delight until his life has been wrecked upon the breakers of some hideous sin. He thought he could stop whenever he willed to do so and under this flattering delusion he blows his dangerous passion into white heat and forges in it link after link in the chain that binds him in its iron grasp at last.

The Entangled Grasshopper

I stood in my back-yard one day and saw a grasshopper hop unwittingly into the web of a huge spider, one of those yellow-backed fellows that makes your flesh creep when you come on them suddenly. And down his silken thread the spider shot, and almost as quickly as I can tell it he rolled that struggling grasshopper over and over like a circus-juggler with a barrel on his feet until the grasshopper found himself wrapped thread after thread in a silken sheet as close winding as an Egyptian mummy.

Habit doesn't work so rapidly but I have seen it slowly, imperceptibly wrap men round and round until they were held as hopelessly in its death-like grip as an Indian tortured victim planted perpendicular-wise in the ground with the earth packed about him even to his lips, and they never knew their bondage until they made their first faint move toward a better life.

No; I have seen a juggler bound hand and foot *shrink* his muscles or by some dexterous turn *loose* his fetters and slip away, but I have never seen a man strong enough or skillful enough to escape the thongs of an evil habit when once he has allowed himself to be caught in its merciless grasp. Where a miracle of faith has rescued one, hundreds have gone down to ignoble ruin and death a slave to the passion they thought they could so easily master. Caught as in the frightful tentacles of a monster devil-fish escape is out of the question; wrapped in the contracting coils of a poisoned-breathed boa-constrictor, the end is quick and sure; bound like another Prometheus to the rock with the black vulture of passion eating at the soul, only the power of God can break the chain.

> *"Habit at first is but a silken thread,*
> *Fine as the light-winged gossamers that sway*
> *In the warm, sunbeams of a summer's day;*
> *A shallow streamlet rippling o'er its bed;*
> *A tiny sappling ere its roots are spread,'*
> *A yet unhardened thorn upon the spray;*
> *A lion's whelp that has not scented prey;*
> *A little smiling child obedient led.*
> *Beware! that thread may bind thee as a chain;*
> *That streamlet gather to a fatal sea;*
> *That sappling spread into a gnarled tree;*
> *That thorn, grown hard, may wound and give thee*
>   *pain;*
> *That playful whelp his murderous fangs reveal;*
> *That child, a giant, crush thee 'neath his heel."*

There is an unwritten saying attributed to Christ by Mohammedan tradition:

"Jesus once said, 'The world is like a deceitful woman who, when asked how many husbands she had, answered, so many that she could not count them. 'I murdered and got rid of them.' 'It is strange' said Jesus, 'that the rest had so little wisdom that, in spite of your cruel treatment of others, they took no warning and still burned with love for you.'"

And it is one of the marvels of iniquity that in spite of the accumulated experience of all the past some people, especially the young of this day, are unwilling to profit by any experience save their own.

Robert Burns, cursed by appetite, confessing he would go to the whiskey-barrel though a loaded cannon were blazing from its top! Lord Byron, at thirty-six, crying,

"The flowers and fruits of love are gone; the worm, the canker and the grief are mine alone!" Gambetta, the brilliant leader of France, dying of putrid and loathesome sores! Edgar Allen Poe, morally insane through the curse of drink, tearing down to his hideous death! — and untold others did time permit their mention — lights of the greatest magnitude, damned by habit; while all around us are hundreds of the more common run, fathers, husbands, and sons; aye, mothers, wives and daughters, too, gone down in the helplessness of despair because they have not been willing to become wise through the experience of the world.

Lacking the Will to Turn

Have I been speaking to any of you this morning? Yes; and I hear you saying "I know what I will do; I will use my volitional power; my will power, and no habit will ever master me."

Well, that's a fine resolution, and I know that men with the proverbial "iron will" have accomplished much. So, resolve; determine; set the teeth; compress the lips; clinch the palms; lower the brow, and say, "By all that's within me, this thing shall not be!" That's the way Hannibal scaled the Alps.

But you say, "What if I can't? This thing is harder than mountain climbing." Yes, wasn't it John Greenleaf Whittier who said,

> "Forever round the mercy-seat
>   The guiding lights of love shall burn;
> But what if, habit-bound, thy feet
>   Shall lack the will to turn?"

"There are three kinds of people in the world," said a writer in one of our magazines some time ago; "the can'ts, the won'ts, and the wills; the can'ts fail in everything; the won'ts oppose everything; the wills accomplish everything." That sounds very good, if it were all true. But there are some things the will alone can't do.

Using the Two Knees

Yet, there is a way. There are times when we must call in the aid of another, and Paul said, "I can do all things through Christ who strengtheneth me." Better than the strongest will is the bending of the knees.

A poor Chinaman, for thirty-nine years a slave to the opium habit, got the victory at last, and when asked how he did it, he said, "I used my two knees." And it is only when we have discovered this secret that the words of the poet are really true:

> *"So near is grandeur to our dust,*
> *So nigh is God to man;*
> *When duty whispers low, 'Thou must,'*
> *The youth replies, 'I can'."*

I cannot explain the mystery of heaven's help; how God's almightiness can flow through my helplessness and make me strong to overcome; but I can recommend my Lord to you.

Young men and young women, I speak to you this morning. I do not know what your peculiar temptation is; I do not know your besetting sin, but I covet for you the power of Christ in your life. Throw yourself on God, and then with God's help gather up all the energies of body, mind and soul and declare everlasting war against every unholy thing that may have fastened, or is even now fastening itself upon you. Give no quarter and ask for none, but let the demons that would undo you understand that it is a fight to a finish, and Christ will see you through.

Courage Invincible

History tells us that Napoleon had planned a magnificent campaign to defeat the Austrians at Marengo. The 20th of May saw his army on the heights of Saint Bernard. He had made awful havoc of his foes, and on the 14th of June, having dispatched Dessaix on the right, he moved forward to consummate his masterly plan. But a few drops of rain had fallen in the gorges of the Alps and the River Po could not be crossed in time, and Napoleon reached the field just in time to see his brave generals beaten and the Old Guard giving way.

Just as the day was lost, Dessaix, the boy general, came sweeping across the field at the head of his cavalry and halted on the hilltop where Napoleon stood. In his corps there was a drummer boy whom Dessaix had picked up on the streets of Paris. He had followed the victorious Eagles of France in the campaigns of Egypt and Germany. As the column halted Napoleon shouted to him, "Gamin, beat a retreat!" The boy did not stir. "Gamin, I say, beat a retreat!" The boy stepped forward and grasped his drum sticks and said, "Sire, I don't know how; Dessaix never taught me that. But I can beat a charge. Oh, I can beat a charge that would make the dead fall into line. I beat that charge at the Pyramids; I beat it at Mt. Tabor, and I beat it again at the Bridge of Lodi; may I beat it here?" Napoleon turned to Dessaix and said, "What shall we do; we are beaten?" "There is time enough yet for a victory," said Dessaix; "the charge! the charge! Let him beat the charge of Lodi and the Pyramids! And a moment later the corps followed the sword gleam of Dessaix, and keeping step to the furious roll of the boy's drum, they swept down on the hosts of Austria. They drove the first line back on the second and the second back on the third, and there they fell like ripened grain before the sickle, but the line never faltered, and when the smoke of battle cleared away the boy was seen in the front of the line marching right on still beating his furious charge.

My young friend, that's the kind of warfare I call you to

this morning in seeking for the mastery of your soul. Doesn't the very thought of it thrill you? You must never learn to beat a retreat.

THE VICTORIOUS FINISH

I saw a picture in one of our galleries of an old derelict of a vessel, an old battered hulk on a rough sea with threatening clouds. No canvas ever spoke with plainer voice its message. I might describe it; I might comment upon it, but down underneath the painting is a verse that tells the whole weird, pathetic story. Listen to the words:

"Storm-beaten, torn and tossed
By night and day.
Lone, Lorn, Lamented, Lost;
Drifting away."

What a picture of many a soul I know and you know. But for you this morning, my young friend, my prayer is that in the struggle for the mastery you may know the sweets of victory here, and the blessing of God's "Well done," hereafter, when the angel of reward, waiting within the pearly gates, shall crown your immortal brow with the diadem of rejoicing which shall never grow dim throughout the ages of a never-ending eternity. "Thanks be unto God who giveth us the victory through our Lord Jesus Christ."

IX
WHAT MUSIC CAN DO

"And it came to pass when the evil spirit from God was upon Saul that David took a harp and played with his hand: So Saul was refreshed and was well, and the evil spirit departed from him." —I SAMUEL 16:23.

D AVID WAS A POET and a musician. He accompanied his instrument with words of his own composition. Nature had filled his soul with its melody in the quiet hours of his pastoral life, while the stirring battle experiences prepared him for the triumphal songs he has left behind.

He has touched with a master hand every chord in the human heart and every melody and aspiration of the human soul. He was a skilled player on stringed instruments. He had a harp and the air was made vocal with richest strains as his practiced fingers swept the keys, and the delicate touch of his master-hand became so notorious throughout the neighborhood that when king Saul, troubled by an evil spirit, said "Provide me now a man that can play well and bring him to me," one of the servants at once mentioned the name of David as one cunning in playing.

Saul wanted some one who could "play well." Some musicians play "too religiously." They obey the Bible injunction and never let their left hand know what their right hand is doing. But David "played well."

Saul had wilfully disobeyed God and God had rejected him as king and his doom pronounced by Samuel sank deep into his soul. David, the shepherd musician, came and standing before the king took a harp and played with his hand, and Saul was so much refreshed that for a time at least the evil spirit departed out of him.

Some one has said that David's harping would sound harsh to an ear trained to the subtle harmonies of a Wagner or a Mozart. That may be true. It may be true that Elijah might not have appreciated the "Elijah" by Mendelssohn. Even the cultured English at first said that it had no melody in it.

Music hath Charms

Nevertheless the ancients were a musical people, especially the Hebrews, and later the Greeks. They were strangely susceptible to the influence of music. David soothed the spirit of Saul and Elisha calls for a minstrel to prepare his mind for prophetic utterances.

Who was it that said, "Music hath charms to soothe the savage beasts"? The Greeks must have believed it, for in one of their most beautiful myths Orpheus is given a lyre by his father Apollo, and so sweetly did he play that nothing could withstand the charm. Even the wild animals thronged entranced about him; the rocks were softened and the knotted oaks were bent. At the death of Eurydice, his beautiful young wife, he followed her down into the realm of Pluto and there sang his woes so pathetically that the ghosts wept, Tantalus forgot his thirst, the Furies shed tears, and Pluto consented to restore Eurydice to him on condition that he lead her forth without looking back upon her. Failing to look straight before him he lost her once more and went forth to sing his complaints, accompanied by his lyre, to the rocks and the mountains, melting the hearts of tigers and charming the oaks from their stations.

The story of David and Saul has its counter-part on every page of history.

After the Massacre of Saint Bartholomew midnight horrors of the brain would not permit Charles the Ninth to sleep save as he was composed to rest by a symphony of singing boys.[1]

The reliable testimony of the French Academy gives among other cases that of a fever-stricken patient suffering violent delirium, cured in six days by the strange power of music over his nerves.

People peculiarly susceptible to the strains of music have fainted from its over-powering effects in the rendition of Handel's "Messiah."

When every other remedy had failed to relieve Philip the Fifth, of Spain, of a fit of despondency and gloom, the Queen thought of music, and Farinelli, a sweet singer, was summoned to sing in an adjoining room, with the effect that the king yielded to its charms, aroused himself from his lethargy and appeared again in the council ready for the affairs of state.

When Washington, to lessen expense, diminished the number of bands, his general, after the first engagement, sent for more music, telling Washington that he had diminished the efficiency of his army.

It was music that cheered the patriots up Bunker Hill. It was music that revived the lagging spirits of Napoleon's army and sent them shouting over the Alps. It was a full band playing "La Marseillaise" at Sebastapol that led the French victoriously against Fort Malakhoff. It was under

---

1. August 23-24, 1572, Roman Catholics in Paris slaughtered thousands of Protestants, known as Huguenots. The massacre spread throughout France, eventually killing 5,000-30,000 people. —Ed., 2016

the inspiration of "Old Hundred," sung by Cromwell's marching thousands, that he led them on to victory.

God at the Organ

Music was born with creation and all nature became instinct with it. "The unbounded universe is one sleepless lyre whose chords of love and of hope, of purity and of peace are fanned into a dreamy, mystic melody by the breath of the invisible God." Every shining orb in the radiant heavens is a celestial key over which the fingers of God swept to create "the music of the spheres," when "the morning stars sang together and all the sons of God shouted for joy."

God loves music. It is one of His best gifts to man. He put that marvelous muscular mechanism in the human throat and lungs; an endowment of forty-four muscles capable of 173,000,000 variations of sound. He calls for the music of the voice, for the psaltery and the harp, for the organ and the ten-stringed instruments.

Music is the language of the soul. It would be a cheerless world without it. Wherever it goes it brightens the world and lifts up the heart of man. It comforts the sorrowing soul. It inspires determination in the face of deepest discouragement. It prepares the soul for its highest and holiest impressions. It fills the heart with better purpose and purer motive. It moulds character.

When Music Fails

No wonder music has held such a place in religious worship in all ages and among all people. And yet music satisfies only for a time. Its helpfulness is only ephemeral. It may for a time cheer up drooping spirits and lift up drooping hearts, but if the soul is ever to be filled with music that will always bring peace in your deepest sorrow, that will always bring comfort in your heaviest trouble, that will always "set the joy-bells ringing in your soul," and drive out every evil spirit it must be the song that is born in the soul by a diviner presence. David must have played strangely sweet and sacred music. I should like to have seen him as he swept the strings of his harp, and heard those beautiful sounds that were so uncongenial to the evil spirit possessing Saul. But, oh, how much poor Saul needed something else.

Saul's heart was alienated from God and a stringed instrument couldn't bring it back; nor could the minstrel's silver tongue discourse music sweet enough to bring it into harmony with God.

Saul was refreshed for a time but still there was discord in his soul that drove him deeper into darkness. His history runs quickly to its end. From the gloomy cave of the Endor witch he goes into hopeless battle, and when the terrible drama is finished the curtain drops before the unhappy king, "his kingdom rent, his children slain, his army lost, himself from hope cast out," throwing himself upon his sword to be his own destroyer.

Saul's trouble was too deep to be reached by musical notes. There is one thing that music cannot do. It cannot cure a sin-sick soul. The root of this disease is too deep. It needs a better antidote than sound-vibrations can ever produce. It needs the "Balm of Gilead." Take music for your physician and its harmonies will fill your soul with the false note of "peace, peace," when there is no peace, but when the Great Physician comes, He enters into the soul and is at once your song and your peace.

On returning from the Crusades, Richard, the Lion-hearted, was captured and imprisoned for many months in a strong castle. No one knew where he was and the English people mourned him as dead. But an old musician of the royal house determined to find him and he went from city to city and from prison to prison and standing in their grim shadows he played and sang an old song that his king had loved in better days. He thought that if the king should hear the sounds he would in some way make it known. At last one day when he had sung for almost an hour before an old castle he saw a hand high up thrust through a grating and wave a white handkerchief and he knew he had found his king, the lost one he so dearly loved. He carried the news to his people and the king was saved.

THE DIVINE ORPHEUS

And so Jesus came to seek and to save that which was lost. Like Orpheus, going down into the Plutonic realm, so Christ came down into a lost world to lead imprisoned souls up to heaven's glory, and if you will make Him one sign that the sweet music of His Gospel invitation has struck one responsive chord in your soul, He will break every prison bar and every chain and lead you "forth out of the bondage of corruption into the glorious liberty of the children of God." He will put a new song of praise in your mouth and fill your soul with His own eternal self which is the harmony of God.

When the organist of the celebrated Freiburg cathedral became old and his fingers had lost their skill he was made custodian and given the charge of caring for the great organ. One day a visitor came into the cathedral and asked permission to play upon the celebrated instrument, but was refused.

"No one," said the custodian, "but myself and the present organist have ever touched those keys."

But after much persuasion the visitor was reluctantly granted permission to play a few notes. He slipped into the seat and touched first one key and then another, and then running his fingers along the keys he filled the whole cathedral with such wonderful music that the old organist was entranced. He stood spell-bound and when the visitor had finished the old man came up beside him and said,

"What might your name be, Sir?"

"My name," replied the visitor, "is Felix Mendelssohn."

And until the end of his life the old organist was used to say, "And I all but missed hearing Mendelssohn play on my organ!"

Oh, my friend, there is One here this morning who is greater than Mendelssohn, waiting permission to play upon the organ of your soul. He is the great soul tuner; the Master Musician. Let Him come in and He will fill your soul with celestial music and tune it into harmony with the harps of heaven, and life will be one long glad anthem, beginning here and now and continuing throughout the never-ending ages of eternity.

I like to think of Heaven as a place of song.

The Man Who had no Song

Did you ever hear of the man who wanted to go to heaven without a song? He knew he was soon to die and the minister had come to see him. When the doctor shakes his head the minister is always welcome, and he asked the man concerning his soul.

"Well," he said, "I think my chances for getting to heaven are pretty good."

"Do you believe there is a heaven?"

"Yes."

"Do you believe there is a hell?"

"Yes, there must be."

"Do you believe your soul is immortal and will soon be forever in one or the other of these two places?"

"Yes," he said earnestly.

"Well, your reason for thinking your chances for heaven are pretty good; would you tell me what it is?"

His answer came slowly as he said:

"Well, I've always been a moral man and respectable; I've been kind to my wife and children, and I have not intentionally wronged any one."

"Well, that's very commendable; but what kind of a place do you think heaven is?"

"I think it is a very happy place, without sin or sorrow, and I think they sing a great deal there."

"Yes, you are right; and do you know the song they sing?"

"No, I had never thought about that."

"Well," said the minister, "I will read it to you."

And turning to Revelation 1:5 he read, "Unto Him that loved us and washed us from our sins in his own blood; to Him be glory and dominion forever and ever."

"You see," said the minister, "they are praising their Saviour, the One who loved them and died for them. They haven't a word to say about what *they* have done; it's all about what *He* has done. *He* loved them and *He* died for them. Now suppose you get to heaven in the way you say — because you have been good to your family and so on; there would be one sinner in heaven who couldn't join in the song they sing; you would be there without a Saviour and you would have no song to sing."

And as if waking out of a dream, he said, "I had never thought of it that way before!" And he became extremely anxious about his soul and wanted to have the question settled at once.

Then turning to I Timothy 1:15, the minister read, "This is a faithful saying and worthy of all acceptation, that Christ Jesus came into the world to save sinners." And the man said:

"That's me; and I want to accept Him now."

He lived but a few days but when the minister came back the man said, with a strange new light of joy in his face,

"I'll have a song now. It will be 'Unto Him that loved us and washed us from our sins in His own blood.'"

He fell into a peaceful sleep, and in a few moments was gone to join the celestial choir as with grateful hearts they make heaven vocal with that glorious anthem which none but the redeemed of the earth can sing.

God grant that when you come to die your soul may be

in harmony with heaven's sweet music, and that you may hear at heaven's portal the beautiful strains of the angels of God singing for you an abundant entrance into the Lamb's bright hall of song.

And when glorified David takes up his golden harp to lead the grand chorus of that celestial host, with melody in our souls and with songs on our lips we will join the countless blood-washed throng in glad Hallelujahs to the Lamb, and Heaven's temple will be filled with music, the entrancing sweetness and power of which no mortal can conceive, and heaven's jasper walls, sparkling with the sunlight of everlasting day, will catch up the strains and echo back in trembling cadence, "Worthy is the Lamb that was slain to receive blessing and riches and honor and glory and power, world without end; Amen and Amen."

And my earnest prayer for you—for each and every one of you—is that you might know the peace, the comfort, and the joy that comes from having a hope like that, born in the soul because of the presence of the glorious son of the most high God.

X
THE GOD WITH A VEILED FACE

"While thy servant was busy here and there, the man was gone." —I KINGS 20:40.

IN ONE OF the cities of ancient Greece was a sculptor who spent much of his time carving statues of the gods. Into his studio there came one day a visitor just as the sculptor was putting the finishing touches upon a rather peculiar piece of work. It was a statue, the hair of whose head was thrown around to cover the face; on each foot there was a wing, and the statue was standing on its toes.

The visitor asked for its name, and the sculptor said it was "Opportunity."

"Why is its face veiled?" he asked.

"Because men seldom know her when she comes to them," was the reply.

"And why does she stand upon her toes, and why the wings?"

"Because," said the sculptor, "when once she is gone she can never be overtaken."

It was this story that gave me the text I have chosen this morning.

Opportunity and the Idle Dreamer

It was in the thick of battle. An officer brought to one of his soldiers an important prisoner. "Guard this man," he said, "with utmost care; upon him depends the issue of the campaign. If by any means he escape, thy life shall be for his." Strangely enough the soldier became careless. His bow and his spear he leaned against the tent. Hungry, he baked a few cakes. Sleepy, he dozed a bit on his elbow. Suddenly a noise startled him and he sprang up just in time to see his prisoner take one leap and disappear into the thicket. A concealed knife had cut the ropes. That night the general returned and as the trembling soldier stood before his master the only thing he could say was: "While thy servant was busy here and there the man was gone."

Gone Opportunity, and lightning cannot equal its flight! Gone forever Opportunity, and the wings of seraphim cannot overtake it and bring it back.

I do not believe with Proctor that,

"No star was ever lost we once have seen;
We always may be what we might have been."

Rather must we say with Browning,

"This could have but happened once;
And we missed it—lost it forever."

There is something strategic in every opportunity that decides for man the forces that are to mould his life.

It was Shakespeare who said,

"There is a tide in the affairs of men which taken
at its flood leads on to fortune; omitted, and all the
voyage of life is bound in shallows and miseries."

The Proverb says, "Strike while the iron is hot." To strike at any other time is useless. Too hard a moment before, it is too hard a moment later.

I do not mean to say that if a man misses an Opportunity he will never have another; scarcely another exactly like it; and that one may have been the supreme Opportunity of his life. There is a strategic time when everything is ripe for action. To neglect that time is to do so at infinite cost.

IT IS SO WITH NATURE. There is a time at which all the forces of nature focalize their generating powers. It is Spring time. You may break up the ground in winter, and sow your seed, but without the warmth of the summer sun and the rain of the summer clouds you will never reap a harvest.

IT IS SO WITH HISTORY. History is full of these strategic times. Such was the time when the Gospel came; one universal language; one universal government; substantial roadways and a thriving commerce. The right hour had struck; the Man of Nazareth appeared and His message went ringing round what was then the world.

IT IS SO WITH THE INDIVIDUAL. For the men who have achieved greatness there was a moment when the tide was at its flood; they caught it and rode out on the majestic billow of success.

There was one very critical hour at Waterloo, big with destiny for nations. But General Blucher came up just one moment too late. Napoleon's star had already set. General Blucher had missed his opportunity, but another man had found his. Nathan Rothchild had watched the struggle from his horse on a neighboring hill and when he saw the French retreat he dashed off to Ostend, paid two thousand francs to cross the channel in a storm and taking advantage of the London markets he counted his gold by the millions.

It is a sad thought indeed, that of an Opportunity lost forever. The door swung noiselessly open but we did not heed the invisible beckon from within, and as noiselessly it closed again. The god with the veiled face passed us by but we did not recognize her, and as the wings of her feet discover her identity the very swiftness with which they fly away seems to say, "Too late; you cannot overtake me now!"

It might have been. In that moment was wrapped the easy possibilities of all that makes life most beautiful, most satisfactory and most useful—but now it is gone and gone forever; for

"THE MILL WILL NEVER GRIND WITH THE WATER THAT IS PAST."

I wonder if it is not true that God has a plan for every man's life—a channel through which He would have it go. Some men strike that channel early in life; some strike it later, and some, alas, never strike it at all, and dying:

"Of all sad words of tongue or pen;
The saddest are these, —'It might have been'."

There are three words I am thinking about this morning. One is "Success"; one is "Service"; and the other is "Salvation."

I. WHAT ABOUT THE OPPORTUNITY FOR SUCCESS?

Some people complain that Opportunity has been partial and given them no chance. But such people, as a rule, are waiting for some extraordinary event; awaiting, like Micawber, for something to "turn up"; for some flood-tide to carry them off their feet.

But Opportunity never comes to an idle dreamer. For after all it is only as we are walking in the path of duty, doing what we believe to be the present will of God for us, that the very Opportunity we need will be found lying close to us in perhaps the simplest and most familiar event that engages our attention.

I am reminded of that interesting legend of an artist who long sought a piece of sandalwood out of which to carve a beautiful Madonna of which he had dreamed. At last he was about to give up in despair and leave the vision of his life unrealized, when in a dream he was bidden to shape the figure from a block of ordinary oak wood which was destined for the fire. He obeyed the command and produced from the log of common firewood a Madonna of surpassing beauty which as his masterpiece won for him great-renown.

"Master of human destinies am I;
Fame, love, and fortune on my footsteps wait."

So sings the poet from the Sunflower State in his master poem, "Opportunity," but the pathetic thing about it all is that so often while a man is busy here and there with the insignificant and trivial affairs that do not count, the god with the veiled face and winged feet sweeps swiftly by, and all unconscious of his heavenly messenger, the man is lost forever to the Opportunity that would have opened for him the door into all that would have put success within his certain grasp and made life for him really worth the living.

A man told me the other day the story of his disappointing career; how he failed to recognize the Opportunity that would have carried him to a place of great worth; and as he talked a tear rolled down upon his pillow, and he said, "That's where I made my mistake; but it's too late now." Yes, it was too late, for

"THE MILL WILL NEVER GRIND WITH THE WATER THAT IS PAST."

II. WHAT ABOUT THE OPPORTUNITY FOR SERVICE.

More and more as the centuries have rolled along have we learned to emphasize the principle of social sympathy and social responsibility. And we do well, for was not the whole existence of our Great Exemplar all the way from the throne of His glory to the Manger of Bethlehem and back again by way of Calvary a continual giving of Himself for you and for me and for the whole world? And did He not constantly enforce in all his teaching the debt which strength owes to weakness? Aye, and when the Judgment for reward takes place is He not to say to those upon His right, "I was hungry and ye fed me; thirsty and ye gave me drink; sick and ye visited me; in prison and ye came unto me," and to those upon His left, "Ye did it not; ye did it not"? And judgment falls accordingly.

God would not have a man become a Dead Sea of accumulated treasure, always getting and never giving. That was a fine motto the old Quaker gave us. He said, "I expect to pass through this life but once; if there is any kindness or any good thing I can do to my fellow being, let me do it now. I shall pass this way but once."

What Life is For

Do you remember the poem entitled, "The House by the Side of the Road," written by Sam Walter Foss about the little old man who lived along the roadside showing always a bit of kindness to his neighbors and the strangers who passed by?

"There are hermit souls that live withdrawn,
In the place of their self-content;
There are souls like stars that dwell apart
In a fellow less firmament.
There are pioneer souls that blaze their paths
Where the highways never ran;
But let me live in a house by the side of the road,
And be a friend to man."

There's more of it and it's all good; but here's something just as good, if not a little better:

"'Tis only half a truth the poet has sung
Of the house by the side of the way;
Our Master had neither a house nor a home
But He walked with the crowd day by day.
And I think when I read of the poets desire,
That a house by the road would be good;
But service is found in its tenderest form,

When we walk with the crowd in the road.

So I say, let me walk with the men in the road,
  Let me seek out the burdens that crush;
Let me speak a kind word of good cheer to the weak
  Who are falling behind in the rush.
There are wounds to be healed, and breaks we must
      mend;
  There's a cup of cold water to give;
And the man in the road by the side of his friend
  Is the man who has learned how to live."

LIFTING THE LOAD TOGETHER

You cannot bear my burden for me. Sometimes it is heavy and the road is rough. But a smile, a kind word, a glad hand does good like a medicine; and as the heart grows braver the burden seems to grow a bit lighter and the road a bit smoother, and both the worth and the issue of my life depends very much upon whether I live it with or without the little kindness and the little love that you can give.

But social responsibility does not end even here. If man is in any sense his brother's keeper, then this profound ethical concept finds its highest interpretation in the spiritual obligation resting upon the professing Christian to share with his brother man the knowledge that makes for eternal life.

And believe me, the saddest moment that can ever come into your life, if you are that professing Christian, will be when some one passes unprepared into the other world, and you are forced to confess that you knew him, called him friend, and yet let slip away a hundred golden opportunities to tell him of your hope.

Well might one wish the wheel of time reversed if such could bring again the Opportunity for such a service that is now gone forever. So often, indeed, it is now or never. Today only is ours. Tomorrow may be too late; for,

"The mill will never grind with the water that is past."

III. And now once more; what about the opportunity for salvation — for soul-security?
This is the saddest thought of all.
Every day men are being hurled into eternity without a moment's warning. But there is something else that ought to concern you. It is this. It is possible for a man to so long refuse to yield himself to the impression of the truth that he loses altogether the capacity for being impressed. This is what Jesus meant when He said of certain people, who had so repeatedly, so persistently refused to believe — He said, "Therefore, they could not believe." They were not able to believe. It was morally impossible.

Above the Temple at Delphi were carved the words, "Know thy opportunity." And I read in this Book, "Now is the accepted time; now is the day of salvation; the day of Opportunity." You may have another. I do not know, but I do know that it will be harder to embrace if it does come because you are rejecting the one you have today.

Trifling with One's Soul

I read the other day of a man who was a skillful juggler. He had vast estates. He sold them and put the proceeds into a pearl of wondrous beauty. He took passage on a ship for sunny Italy intending to buy an old vineclad castle, surround himself with servants and spend his last years in ease and comfort. He had made for his pearl a rosewood jewelled casket locked with a golden lock and a golden key.

A boy was selling apples on the deck. He borrowed two, three, five, up to nine and tossed them into the air and kept them shining there with his wonderful skill. The passengers were charmed and gave him great applause. He said, "Thank you, ladies and gentlemen, but this is no test of my skill. Wait." He hurried to his cabin, opened the rosewood casket and took the pearl from its velvety nest.

He hurried back to the deck and said, "Look!" and tossed it high into the air. It sparkled in the sunlight like a blazing coal. It came straight down and he had it in his hand.

"What is it?" said the ladies, and as he passed it to them they were charmed by its beauty.

"How much is it worth?" they said.

"Worth?" said he, "Why, my whole vast fortune is wrapped up in that stone."

"Well, then for goodness sake don't trifle with it that way!"

"Oh," he said, "there's no danger. Look!" and this time he leaned out over the railing and tossed the precious thing again into the air, and again he caught it and said, "Here it is!"

A lady screamed and said, "Man don't be a fool; give me the pearl and play with this apple if you want to further demonstrate your skill."

But he laughed and said, "My eyes are as keen as an eagle's. My nerves are true as the needle to its pole. Now look!" And this time leaning farther out he threw it higher than ever before. Down it came but just as it touched his hand the ship gave a lurch, and down into the fathomless depths went his pearl. "Lost," he cried, "everything I have in this world is gone. What a fool I have been to trifle with a fortune and risk my all simply for the plaudits of a passing crowd."

My friend, if you ever lose your soul, it will be just that way, because you have played with it and trifled away every opportunity to redeem it.

Oh man, what is your life? If you had been born a beast, some winged creature of the air, or creeping thing of the ground, you could not have lived for a less noble purpose than some of us are living today; while the sun in its race and the stars in their path are shedding their beams to light us on our way to that dismal ending where no ray of light ever enters and no star of hope ever shines.

May God help us to so number our days that we may apply our hearts unto wisdom. For

"The mill will never grind with the water that is past."

XI
LIFE'S MOST IMPORTANT QUESTION —
WHAT MUST I DO TO BE SAVED?

"Believe on the Lord Jesus Christ and thou shalt be saved."
—ACTS 16:30.

EOPLE WHO DON'T WANT any sensation connected with religion ought to give this incident a wide berth. If ever there was an exciting time it was when the Philippian jailer got converted.

There are a good many Church people who are mightily scared about a little excitement when it is connected with religion, but these same people will yell like maniacs on the Board of Trade, or throw a fit of frenzied enthusiasm over almost anything else that interests them if there is only half an occasion for it.

If the people who complain of extravagant gestures and pulpit enthusiasm in general would read history they would discover some worthy exemplars of such style in many of the greatest preachers the world has ever known.

A contemporary of John Knox said that even in his old age, when he had to be helped up the pulpit stairs, he would soon be preaching with such extreme vehemence that *"he was likely to ding the pulpit into blads and flee out of it."*

The people of Wotton called Rowland Hill a madman, and he said in his defense, "While I passed along yonder road I saw a gravel-pit cave in and bury three men alive. I hastened to the rescue and shouted for help till they heard me in the town almost a mile away. Nobody called me a madman then. But when I see destruction about to fall on sinners and entomb them in an eternal mass of woe, and I cry aloud, if perchance they may behold their danger and escape, they say I am beside myself; perhaps I am," he said. But people, listen, if this is what it means to be a madman, then God hasten the day when our pulpits will be filled with maniacs.

How the Philippian Jailer was Converted

Now I want to tell you how the conversion of the Philippian jailer came about. Paul and Silas were well known on the streets of Philippi, and one day a demon-possessed girl cried after them in mockery and Paul rebuked the evil spirit within her and the girl became herself again. But there was a little group of degenerate rascals who had been coining the poor girl's shame into money, and *"when they saw that their hope of gain was gone"* the promoters of the brutal and devilish traffic laid hold on Paul and Silas and hustled them off to the Chief Magistrate, to the Mayor of the city, and this little machine politician, who doubtless held his office at the hands of the gang, ordered them to be beaten and sent to jail.

It says *"The jailer thrust them into the inner prison and made their feet fast in the stocks."* Jails are miserable enough now, but in those days they were something fierce. Come along with me and let us pay a visit to the Philippian jail. It's midnight, but you would never know it; for in the dungeons it is always midnight. I have been in these dungeons. The chill and the odor of the damp, foul air are with me this morning again in memory.

Now, listen to the heart-sickening sounds; the groan of poor victims who have not seen the sunlight for years; the cough of the consumptive wasting away; the wail of despair; the deep sigh; the clanking chains of some poor culprit as he rolls over in his dreams; the shriek of some poor soul in a nightmare of horror, and the curses of those who are crying out against their cruel fate, and you say, "God pity the poor prisoners!"

But now, listen; some one is singing; singing praises to God; and now they are praying. And we say,

"Jailer, these are strange sounds for a place like this where everybody else is groaning and cursing; come, take us to them."

And in a moment we are standing in front of two prisoners, sitting on the cold ground, their backs running blood from a recent beating, their feet fastened tight in wooden sockets. And we say,

"Jailer, why have you got these two men here?"

And he says, "I didn't mean to put them here but I was commanded and had to do it. No such prisoners ever came into this dungeon before. They said, 'Good evening, Jailer,' when they came in; their faces wore a look that has tarried with me since the hour they entered, and while I made their feet fast in the stocks they talked to me about a strange new hope, and I have been much disturbed in my soul."

But while in imagination we stand there in the gloom of that dungeon, suddenly there is a great earthquake. It is God's Amen to Paul's prayer. Some people don't believe that prayers are answered, but here is one that was answered with a bang.

The foundations of the old jail commence to rock; the iron bars begin to twist; the doors burst open and every prisoner's bonds are loosed. It was a Roman law that if the prisoner escaped the jailer would forfeit his own life as a penalty; so he drew his sword and was about to fall upon it when Paul cried, "Stop! Stop! Do thyself no harm; we are all here." And when he saw that Paul had spoken the truth he fairly rushes up to the two itinerant preachers and out of the depths of a troubled and yet grateful heart he cries, "Sirs, what must I do to be saved?"

LIFE'S MOST IMPORTANT QUESTION

"What must I do to be saved?" Of all the questions ever uttered by the human soul there is not one in all the universe of God in the answer to which are involved such tremendous issues for time and for eternity.

Now what did Paul have to say? He gave that trembling jailer one compact, thrilling, tremendous answer. He told him what to do. What did he tell him?

DID HE TELL HIM TO TAKE A COURSE IN PSYCHOLOGY? No. Psychoanalyzing the soul may show you what a strange bug you are but it can never "sprinkle the heart of an evil conscience."

DID HE TELL HIM TO CHANGE HIS ENVIRONMENT? No. If your watch doesn't run it will do no good to take it out of your pocket and hang it on a rose bush. It needs fixing up on the inside.

DID HE TELL HIM TO GIVE UP HIS BAD HABITS AND BECOME RESPECTABLE? No. That is only reformation. It's like whitewashing a rotten post or tying artificial flowers on an everblooming bougainvillea vine.

DID HE TELL HIM TO FOLLOW HIS CONSCIENCE? No. Conscience may be seared and permit a man to become a fiend without protest.

DID HE TELL HIM TO GO AND JOIN THE CHURCH? No. Going into Church doesn't make a Christian any more than going into the insane asylum makes a maniac.

Well, what did Paul tell him to do? Just one thing. He said, *"Believe on the Lord Jesus Christ and thou shalt be saved."*

What Believing Means

And, now, what does that mean? Well, it is not the same thing as believing something *about* Him. To believe something *about* a man is merely the result of a mental operation. To believe *on* a man is to put your confidence in him and trust him for what he can do for you. When the Bible says "believe," it always means in this sense—in the sense of confidence and trust. What Paul is talking about here is "faith." He is telling the Philippian jailer to put his faith in the Lord Jesus Christ. Faith and belief, in the sense of confidence, are synonymous.

Now, there is only one kind of faith. Get that settled right in the beginning. It's the same kind of faith that you exercise every day in regard to the actions of your whole life. There are different degrees of faith but it is of the same kind, and it is at the bottom, at the basis, of all commercial, all social, and all domestic life, and controls practically everything you do.

You would have a very queer experience and a very disappointing time if you moved about with no faith in anybody. You would go to your office in the morning hungry because you have no faith that your wife will prepare you any breakfast. She said she would, but that is another matter. If you went to the hotel you would leave the meal untouched because you are not sure the proprietor does not mean to poison you. You have a killing pain, but you suffer on because you are suspicious of the surgeon. You want to go north and you start for the station, but you stop on the way because you have no faith in the management's word that they will run the train as the schedule says they will.

The Banker Talks

"Oh," says the banker, "you preachers are impracticable; you are too visionary; you talk too much about faith;

that doesn't interest the business man except for a few minutes on Sunday morning." But how long could a banker run his bank if it wasn't for faith? And every time a man makes a deposit in the bank he is exercising faith in the banker—faith in his ability to wisely invest the funds, and faith in his character that he won't hurry off with them to Canada or to Greece. And it takes a lot of faith, believe me, in these days.

Now, let me say it again; believing without trusting is no faith at all. It begins and ends in a mere mental process. Faith, in the ultimate, is an act of the will.

I may believe the banker to be a good financier and an honest man. I show my faith in the banker when I push my money under the wire wicket.

I may believe the doctor is able to cure me. I show my faith in the doctor when I trust my case to his care.

I may believe that a ship is sea-worthy and can carry me over the water to Europe. I show my faith in the ship when I go on board to make the trip.

I may believe that Christ is able to do for me all that He says He will do. I show my faith in Christ when by an act of my will I trust myself to Him for that purpose.

You say, "Is it as simple as that?" Yes, thank God, it is just as simple as that.

His Wonderful Name

In some passages the Son of God is called "The Lord"; in others He is called "Jesus," and then again He is called "Christ"; but when Paul answered the jailer's question he brought all three names together and said, "Believe on the Lord Jesus Christ and thou shalt be saved."

1. *In the order we think of it we are to believe on Him first of all as "Jesus."*

He is called "Jesus" to emphasize His redemptive office.

"Thou shalt call His name Jesus, for He shall save His people from their sins."

It is God's law we have broken—ten thousand times we have broken it—and God is the only one who can remit the penalty or provide for it. Wink at it? Be indifferent to it? Let it go without penalty? Ordinary intelligence ought to tell us that God could never do a thing like that. God is a righteous God and a holy God as well as a loving Father. Mercy says, "Let the sinner go," but Justice, which is just as essential to the nature of God as mercy, says, "No, it can't be done."

And what did He do? He lifted the sentence of death from my soul by coming Himself in the person of His glorious Son, and, baring His bosom to the deadly shafts of my sin, He made Himself the suffering Lamb of God to bear it away. And thus He became my Saviour.

No wonder Billy Bray, the Cornish miner, saved from the sinful life he was leading, said, when rebuked for shouting Hallelujah, "If they shut me up in a barrel, I'd shout 'Hallelujah' through the bunghole."

2. *Then we are to believe in Him as Lord.*
HE IS CALLED THE LORD TO EMPHASIZE HIS KINGLY OFFICE.

As your Lord He must, of course, rule your life. But a king, if he has the power to do it, protects his subjects. And our King is all-powerful, and I like to think of Him not only as a Saviour but as a Keeper. Mighty to save and able to keep.

3. *And then we are to believe on Him as Christ.*
HE IS CALLED CHRIST TO EMPHASIZE HIS PRIESTLY OFFICE.

He is the Anointed One of God, and as the Great High Priest He is standing just now before the throne of God interceding for all who believe on Him, and pleading for them the merits of His atoning sacrifice when He went upon the Cross for you and me and for all the world.

I wish we might stop just now and sing that wonderful song, "Hallelujah, what a Saviour!" A Jesus who redeems; a Lord whose arm is swift as a ray of light to help me when my feet commence to slip, and if I should go down, a Christ to stand before God and make it right. "Believe on the Lord Jesus Christ and thou shalt be saved."

The Story of von Winkelreid

The story of Arnold von Winkelreid is old but is so thrilling and so inspiring that it must not be forgotten. A great army was marching through Switzerland and everywhere its path was marked with blood and the ghastly ruin of war.

The Swissmen, rich-veined with patriotic blood, had gathered from the mountains and the valleys to fight for their homes and their fatherland. But they were untrained and armed only with whatever weapon they had found and they could not break the well-formed phalanx of the enemy as they marched close together behind their shields and threatening spears, and the Swiss said: "We are lost; our homes must perish and our land go into bondage."

Then Arnold von Winkelreid stepped out and he said: "Men of Switzerland listen to me!"

And they said, "What will *you* do?"

And he said, "This day I will give my life for my country. In yonder valley lies a happy home where wife and children await my return, but they shall see me no more. Follow me," he cried, "I will break the lines and then do your duty and fight every man as best he can and Switzerland will be free." And single-handed and alone he sprang forward, and right where the spears were thickest he ran and shouted as he ran, "Make way for liberty; Make way for liberty."

A hundred gleaming spears were turned to catch him on their points but as he gathered them up in his breast the enemy broke its ranks and through the gap made by his gallant sacrifice the Swiss poured in terrific onslaught and won at last a battle the like of which the world had never heard.

No wonder when you go to Switzerland today and mention the name of Arnold von Winkelreid that the faces of the people of those world-famed hills and valleys will light up and their eyes will fill with tears because of his blessed memory.

But there was One, two thousand years ago, who did a grander thing than that and whose sacrifice set a whole world free. All the powers and principalities of evil were lined up against us and the hosts of Satan, black-pinioned from hell, held us at their mercy. Every method of attack had failed. Every divine maneuver for our rescue had been thwarted, and humanity, sinful and weak, stood hopeless and undone.

Then Jesus, our Lord and Christ, stepped out and the hosts of heaven said, "What will you do?"

And He said, "I will this day give my life for the world."

And He came and said to the battered and besieged sons of men, "Follow me, and I will break the lines; and then, do your duty, every man as best he can, and you shall all be free."

And single-handed, with the instrument of His death, He rushed upon the ranks of hell, and into His own bosom, where dwelt the soul of God, He gathered all the fiery darts that hell could hurl and opened the way of salvation for all who will follow Him. Will you believe on Him and follow Him today?

XII
THE RESURRECTION TRIUMPH

"O Death, where is *thy sting? O Grave, where* is *thy victory?"* —I CORINTHIANS 15:55.

AN UNWELCOME VISITOR

A KNOCK at the door!
"Who's there?"
"I am; Death."
"But I didn't send for you."
"I know you didn't, but I've come, and you must go with me."
"But I'm not ready to go."
"You've had all your life to get ready. Come; you have only three minutes."
"But I can't go. Don't come so close to me. Don't breathe your cold breath in my face."
"One minute; ten seconds; five, four, three, two, one."
And the undertaker is on his way.

Why is death such an unwelcome visitor? Is there anything that can steal away its terrors? anything that can rob it of its sting? Nothing is more dreaded and yet nothing is more certain. It is life's one thing inevitable. What if we were to say it is a blessing in disguise? In a very certain sense that is true.

Somewhere I recall reading a legend like this: A very poor woman, whose name was Misery, lived alone in a little hut. Close by the door was a pear tree that furnished her a living, but she had trouble with the boys who were constantly stealing the fruit.

One day the Lord, Christ, walked the earth in the garb of poverty and no one would entertain Him. He knocked at the door of the rich and the poor but no one would receive Him. At last He came to the hut of Misery and she took Him in, gave Him of her pears to eat, warmed Him by her fire and sat up all night that He might use her pillow. And in the morning He told her that He was the owner of the universe and that He would give her anything she asked. Her only request was that her pear tree might be protected and that whoever climbed up into it might not be able to come down again without her consent, and the request was granted.

One day Death came and told the poor old woman that she must go with him. But she did not want to go. No matter how poverty stricken, no one wants to go with Death. But she said, "I will gladly go if you will be obliging enough to climb up in my pear tree and bring me down a few pears before I start." This Death consented to do, but when once up in the tree he could not come down.

And then troubles came to the world thick and fast. The physicians had no patients; the undertakers had no funerals; the lawyers had no wills to make, and none to break. The young men had no chance, for all the professions and all the occupations were filled with those who got in first and stayed there because Death never took any of them out. Then the earth became overcrowded. No one left it and millions were coming daily into it, and from every quarter of the earth the cry went up for Death, "O Death, where are you?" At last they came to Misery and besought the old woman to let Death come down from the tree, and this she consented to do on condition that he never molest her—that he never take her away. And on this condition Death came down, and this is why we always have Misery with us.

This allegory was evidently written, at least in part, to set forth the thought expressed a moment ago, namely, that Death, in a certain sense, may be looked upon as a blessing in disguise, and that one of the mightiest mercies of this earth is the necessity laid upon man to quit it.

In the text we have chosen death is represented as a venomous serpent and the grave as a formidable conqueror. Death as a serpent has indeed its venom and its sting. It enters alike the palace and the hovel. Today it is the laughing child, tomorrow the ambitious youth, and again the one whose shoulders are bent with years that must succumb to the stroke of this deadly enemy of life. Kings and conquerors are alike weak in its presence. The grave, too, can boast its victories, for what are these mausoleums and monuments and scattered bones on every side but the silent trophies of those whom it has slain.

But Paul speaks of death as a serpent that has lost its sting. It can hiss against him but it cannot harm him. Its teeth have been pulled; its fangs have been jerked out; its stinger is gone. The grave, too, he says, has lost its victory. Its triumph has been snatched away. He really becomes hilarious about the matter, and without fear he despises the injuries of death and treads with triumph upon the earth that he knows must one day cover his lifeless form.

Now where did Paul get his conception of death and the grave that made it possible for him even to rejoice before them and to shout in their presence, "O death, where is thy sting; O grave where is thy victory?"

There are two sources only from which a man may get assurance of any sort; two grounds only which may form the basis of his conclusions. One is Reason and the other is Revelation. Certainly Paul was not satisfied alone with what Reason has to say about the matter under consideration.

REFLECTIONS OF PHILOSOPHY

What does Reason say? Ask the philosopher as did the ancients. And when philosophy had ransacked the whole magazine of its resources it gave a man usually three consolations. And its message is no different today.

1. *It tells us that Death is inevitable and that it is irrational to be disquieted about that which is unavoidable.* A wise man will not fret himself at necessity.

But what comfort is there in this? It is exactly this—the inevitability of death that makes it so terrible. Think you that you can comfort some pitiful wretch by telling him that he must necessarily be miserable and wretched! No. Reason must do something better than that if we are to voice in our own soul the triumphant words which Paul used in giving us our text.

2. *And so philosophy speaks again and this time we are reminded of what a cluttered-up place this earth would be if none of the millions born into it ever left it.* It's like a great ship freighted with mountains and minerals, with oceans and seas and cities, and a passenger list of nearly two billion souls. Thirty millions get on board every year—64 every minute. What if no one ever got off? What was the cause of that frightful disaster a few years ago when the Great Eastern went down? Too many passengers. No ship or no train can continually take on passengers if every one who occupies a berth or a seat never leaves it.

And if Death had never come into this world, unless God had some other plan to get us out, we would be in a fix a million times worse, the philosopher tells us, than anything the Malthusian law of population ever pictured for us.

That all sounds reasonable enough. But even so, most men would prefer to let the other fellow die and get out of the way. And so we will ask philosophy to try again.

3. *And this time it tells us of the freedom brought by Death from the miseries and the troubles and from the sufferings of this life.* Death ends all these things, we are told. So why not welcome it as a shelter-harbor when it comes.

Well, there are some people who look at it that way. In fact, there are not a few who do not even wait for it to come, but voluntarily make for it as a port of refuge when beaten by the tempests and the disastrous storms of life.

One hundred and twenty thousand have done this in this land alone in the last ten years. But when a man blows out his brains to get out of his trouble, he's very sure to find himself in trouble of a more serious kind, that is, if he had full possession of his brains when he did it.

No, there is little if any comfort in such advice.

Most people calculate otherwise. There are millions who seemingly live only to suffer and yet they cling tenaciously to life as the ivy clings to the wall. They are willing to compound for their being by the troubles they must carry. And even when despair has driven them to desperation they are much like the weary traveler in the apologue, who, sinking under his burden, cried for Death to come and ease him; but when Death appeared so grim and ghastly and demanded harshly why he called for him the poor man meekly replied that it was only to help him up with his load again. No, Paul never uttered the shout in our text for a reason like that. And so we will ask Philosophy to try once more. And this time it brings to us the best it has to offer.

4. *Philosophy does bring to a dying man a little hope of future glory.* The soul of the meanest man has ever been instinct with the hope of Immortality.

> *"They that in barbarian burials killed the slave and*
> *slew the wife,*
> *Felt within themselves the sacred passion of the second*
> *life."*

Plato made three strong arguments for immortality the raft on which he sailed through life hoping for the glory of the Elysian Fields beyond. But if the philosophy that argues immortality could only argue as well the happy condition of every man who enters into it, it might relieve somewhat our dread and our anxiety over the prospect of death. But this is just the thing it cannot do. The conscience of every man discovers to him every day the guilt for which reason can discover no atonement. And so, instead of being armed by reason against the fear of death, it argues us, when pursued to its most logical consequence, into eternal woe by proving us wilful transgressors of the law of God which Paul tells us has been written in every man's heart.

And because this is so, what have we seen? We have seen the people of this world, who have been strangers to the Gospel that caused Paul to give us our text, endeavoring by strange illustrations and most horrid methods to expiate their guilt, and to appease the angry gods, even by the sacrifice of human life itself.

No, beloved of God, it was not because of anything philosophy had to say about it that Paul shouted "O Death, where is thy sting; O Grave, where is thy victory." Reason alone can offer no worthy panacea for the gloomy foreboding of the silent messenger so universally dreaded.

THE SURE WORD OF REVELATION

Where then did Paul get the knowledge and what was that knowledge that robbed Death of its sting and the Grave of its victory? He got it, of course, from Revelation, backed up by reason, and it was the knowledge, out of which grew the assurance and the certain expectation of a coming, glorious resurrection that made provision not alone for the reasoned immortality of the soul but the immortality of the body as well, founded upon the indisputable fact that "Christ is now risen from the dead and become the first-fruits of them that sleep." "Wherefore," says Paul, "comfort ye one another with these words; that ye sorrow not as others who have no hope."

Men and women, hear me; I don't know where you are going to find anything that will make you not only unafraid but glad as you contemplate Death and the Grave unless you get it in the way Paul did. Nothing else can do it for you.

I have stood, as you have stood, in the presence of many of the world's illustrious tombs; that surpassing monument of bell-shaped magnificence, overlaid with plates of gold one-eighth of an inch thick, the most sacred spot in the world to millions of Buddhists as the resting place of their beloved Buddha; that far-famed Taj Mahal of Princess Arjamand on the banks of the river Jumna at Agra; that magnificent mausoleum of black Egyptian marble built for Napoleon in Paris; that imposing structure of glittering marble at Mount Vernon, and at Springfield, and on the river-drive at New York, where rest the physical remains of the immortal Washington, Lincoln, and Grant. Hallowed places these all, but the Christian world, thank God, rejoices this morning in *an empty grave!* Death could not hold the Mighty Conqueror! And because He lives, we too shall live.

Oh, for the sweet breath of Easter to sweep over our spirits this morning! The skies smile and the birds sing and the flowers bloom, and all life is bursting forth in Springtime glory, and the whole world does well to celebrate with song, and lilies and roses, and congratulations the resurrection of Him who took the sting out of Death and despoiled the Grave of its victory, and our own resurrection when time shall have come to its end, and "the trumpet shall pour through the flying clouds the harmonies that shall wake the dead."

"In My Father's House"

This whole universe is our Father's house. We are living now in but one of its rooms. There are better rooms upstairs—better light, better air, and better beauty. Man has been called the noblest handiwork of God. So far, Yes, but God didn't half try when He gave us the body we have now.

Better eyes await us. Here we can scarcely see to read; over there we will see from world to world. Better ears—here we hear a few feet off; over there we will listen the whole celestial equator round. Better feet—here two hours at the Century of Progress[1] wear them out; over there they will walk and run and never be weary. Better brains—here we are only picking up pebbles on the beach of truth; over there we will explore the infinite deeps. Richer beauties for the eyes; finer music for the ears; grander truths for the mind; holier errands for the feet. No suffering to be endured; no sorrow, no sickness, no death and no grave and no separation of loved ones forevermore.

Why should we paint death as such a frightful monster if he does all this for us? Why think of him as the king of terrors? Why tremble as we hear him knocking? Why regret that our loved ones are not here? They are walking with the redeemed along the streets of glory. They are fellowshipping with saints celestial in the drawing room of God's eternal mansion. They have heard Moses tell how the waters of the Red sea rolled back for Israel's passage; and Elijah, how the chariot of fire whirled him up into the city where he found the streets were paved with gold; and Daniel, how the lions in their

---

1. Chicago World's Fair, 1933-1934. —*Ed., 2016*

den became his friends; and Peter, how an angel of the Lord drew back for him the bars of his dungeon door; and Paul, how he was caught up into the third heaven and was sent back with his finger on his lips; and John, the beloved, how he saw the Holy City coming down out of heaven from God; and John Knox, and Wesley, and Chalmers and McCheyne, and Moody, and hosts of others of whom the world was not worthy.

Out into a fellowship like that they have gone, and into a reunion with loved ones who went before them, and where together they talk about us, as we talk about absent friends, and wonder when we will come. And every tread on the sapphire steps, every sound at the pearly gate makes their hearts leap, and they say, "We wonder if they are coming now." "O Death, where is thy sting; O Grave, where is thy victory?"

You know Jesus never preached a funeral sermon. He broke up three funerals—the only ones He ever attended. The widow's son, the ruler's daughter, and Lazarus all came back to life at the command of His voice.

The House Eternal

So far as death is concerned He would have us believe that men die only to live. It is only moving into a better place. Knowing that in a few hours He would be dying on the Cross, He said to His disciples, "It is expedient that I go away." Just a going away, as if He were moving to some other city. Moving into better quarters, as Paul puts it. He says, if the house in which you live begins to age, the woodwork to decay, and the masonry to crumble, and the whole structure totter into ruin, you do not remain to perish with it. No, you pack up and move to a better house. "If the earthly house of this tabernacle be dissolved, we have a building of God, a house not made with hands, eternal in the heavens."

Well might Browning, in his closing years, write

"Grow old along with me,
  The best is yet to be—
The last, for which the first was made."

And well might Tennyson, close to the western horizon, sing

"Twilight and evening bell,
  And after that the dark!
And may there be no sadness of farewell
  When I embark;
For though from out our bourne of time and place
  The flood may bear me far,
I hope to see my Pilot face to face
  When I have crossed the bar."

It was on Easter Sunday that Ponce de Leon first came upon this coast. Easter Sunday in Spanish is "Pascua Florida." And that is why this land of sunshine and flowers is called "Florida."

You have stood, most of you, I trust all of you at the empty tomb of Christ, and know that He came out of it. And when another Easter comes along if we are not here we shall be in another city whose name is Beautiful, and we shall wake the Easter music on the flower-strewn fields of Paradise, and hear that great eternal voice say again, "I am the resurrection and the life," and we shall look upon the face of Him, whose face to behold makes Easter leap into eternal rapture and peace, aye, into the sweetness of celestial fellowship forevermore.

www.ingramcontent.com/pod-product-compliance
Lightning Source LLC
Chambersburg PA
CBHW070811050426
42452CB00011B/1986